# Start and Run a Restaurant Business

Brian Cooper, Brian Floody, and Gina McNeill

**Self-Counsel Press**
*(a division of)*
International Self-Counsel Press
USA     Canada

*Copyright © 2000; 2005 by International Self-Counsel Press Ltd.*

*All rights reserved.*

*No part of this book may be reproduced or transmitted in any form by any means — graphic, electronic, or mechanical — without permission from the publisher, except by a reviewer who may quote brief passages in a review.*

*Self-Counsel Press acknowledges the financial support of the Government of Canada through the Book Publishing Industry Development Program (BPIDP) for our publishing activities.*

*Printed in Canada.*

*First edition: 2000; Reprinted: 2002*

*Second edition: 2005*

**Library and Archives Canada Cataloguing in Publication**

Cooper, Brian

    Start & run a restaurant business / Brian Cooper, Brian Floody, and Gina McNeil. — 2nd ed.

    (Self-counsel business series)
    First ed. published under title: Start and run a profitable restaurant.
    ISBN 1-55180-632-0

    1. Restaurant management.  2. New business enterprises--Management. I. Floody, Brian II. McNeill, Gina  III. Title. IV. Title: Start and run a restaurant business. V. Cooper, Brian.  Start and run a profitable restaurant. VI. Series.

TX911.3 M27C65 2005          647.95'068          C2005-900994-2

**Self-Counsel Press**
*(a division of)*
International Self-Counsel Press Ltd.

| 1704 North State Street | 1481 Charlotte Road |
|---|---|
| Bellingham, WA  98225 | North Vancouver, BC  V7J 1H1 |
| USA | Canada |

# Contents

| | | |
|---|---|---|
| **Introduction** | | xiii |
| **Part I: Evaluating Your Dream** | | 1 |
| **1** | **Before You Start** | 5 |
| | 1. The restaurateur as entrepreneur and entertainer | 5 |
| | 2. The menu | 6 |
| | 3. Trends | 7 |
| | 4. Types of restaurants | 8 |
| |    4.1 The gourmet- or fine-dining room | 8 |
| |    4.2 The family, mid-size, casual restaurant | 9 |
| |    4.3 The quick-service or fast-food restaurant | 10 |
| |    4.4 Social and contract caterers | 10 |
| **2** | **The Structure of Your Business** | 11 |
| | 1. The sole proprietorship | 11 |
| |    1.1 Advantages | 12 |
| |    1.2 Disadvantages | 12 |
| | 2. The partnership | 13 |
| |    2.1 Advantages | 13 |
| |    2.2 Disadvantages | 14 |
| | 3. The corporation | 15 |
| |    3.1 Advantages | 16 |
| |    3.2 Disadvantages | 16 |

| | | |
|---|---|---:|
| | 4. Franchising | 17 |
| | 5. Building your team | 20 |
| **3** | **The Business Plan: Feasibility Study** | **23** |
| | 1. The business plan: Overview | 23 |
| | 2. The feasibility study | 26 |
| | 2.1 Target area analysis | 28 |
| | 2.2 Population profile | 28 |
| | 2.3 Economic profile | 31 |
| | 2.4 Competition analysis | 31 |
| | 2.5 Industry and tourism profile | 33 |
| | 2.6 Cultural, recreational, and sporting events | 33 |
| | 2.7 The real estate marketplace | 34 |
| | 3. Pre-opening marketing strategy | 34 |
| **4** | **The Business Plan: The Financial Plan** | **37** |
| | 1. The capital budget | 38 |
| | 1.1 Hard costs | 38 |
| | 1.2 Soft costs | 42 |
| | 2. Investment plan | 45 |
| | 3. Financial statements | 46 |
| | 3.1 The income statement | 46 |
| | 3.2 The break-even analysis | 52 |
| | 3.3 The balance sheet | 54 |
| | 3.4 The cash-flow analysis | 54 |
| | 4. Resources | 56 |
| **Part II: Start-Up** | | **59** |
| **5** | **Start-Up Practicalities** | **63** |
| | 1. Naming your restaurant | 63 |
| | 1.1 Your own tastes | 63 |
| | 1.2 Marketing implications | 64 |
| | 1.3 Copyright | 64 |

| | | |
|---|---|---|
| 2. | Registering your business | 65 |
| | 2.1 In the United States | 65 |
| | 2.2 In Canada | 66 |
| 3. | Trademarks | 66 |
| 4. | Obtaining licenses and permits | 66 |
| 5. | Insurance | 67 |

**6 Choosing Your Restaurant's Location** — 69

| | | |
|---|---|---|
| 1. | Finding the fit | 69 |
| 2. | Downtown versus suburban | 71 |
| | 2.1 Suburban | 71 |
| | 2.2 Downtown/city | 72 |
| 3. | Freestanding versus mall location | 72 |
| 4. | Zoning | 73 |
| 5. | Leasing versus purchasing | 73 |

**7 Design and Renovation** — 77

| | | |
|---|---|---|
| 1. | Building your dream | 77 |
| 2. | What designers can do for you | 78 |
| 3. | Design | 78 |
| 4. | Decor | 81 |
| 5. | Designing without a designer | 81 |
| 6. | A word about renovation | 82 |

**8 Equipment and Furnishings** — 85

| | | |
|---|---|---|
| 1. | Equipment | 85 |
| | 1.1 Sourcing equipment | 86 |
| | 1.2 New versus used equipment | 87 |
| | 1.3 Buy versus lease equipment | 88 |
| | 1.4 Kitchen equipment | 88 |
| | 1.5 Front-of-the-house equipment | 89 |
| 2. | Furnishings | 90 |
| | 2.1 Tables | 90 |
| | 2.2 Chairs | 93 |
| | 2.3 Other furnishings | 93 |

|  |  | 2.4 | Kitchen/bar small wares | 93 |
|  |  | 2.5 | Dinnerware (china, flatware, glassware, linen) | 95 |

**9 Your Employees** — 101

1. Job analysis, job description, and job specifications — 102
2. Recruitment — 104
3. Selection — 105
4. Orientation and training — 108
5. Policy and procedure manuals — 109
6. Reward and discipline — 112
7. Performance appraisals — 113
8. Pay scales — 114
9. Management communications — 114
   9.1 Log books and incident and accident reports — 118
   9.2 Managers' meetings — 118

**Part III: Managing Your Operation** — 121

**10 Your Menu** — 125

1. Types of menus — 126
2. Menu pricing — 127
3. Menu design and development — 128
4. Developing a wine list — 131
   4.1 Wine pricing — 133
   4.2 Designing your wine list — 133
   4.3 Resource guide — 136

**11 The Art of Service** — 137

1. Keeping customers satisfied — 137
2. Service styles — 138
3. Front-of-the-house considerations — 140
4. Dealing with difficult customers — 141

**12 Marketing** — 143

1. Ongoing marketing strategies — 144
   1.1 Advertising — 144

|  |  |  |
|---|---|---|
| | 1.2 Sales | 147 |
| | 1.3 Merchandising | 147 |
| | 1.4 Public relations | 148 |
| | 1.5 Promotions | 149 |
| 2. | Professionals, and what they have to offer | 150 |
| | 2.1 Sourcing the pros | 151 |
| 3. | Building your marketing base | 152 |
| | 3.1 A loyal customer is free advertising | 153 |
| | 3.2 The role of service in marketing | 154 |
| 4. | Increasing sales by using the five "Ps" of marketing | 155 |
| | 4.1 Product | 156 |
| | 4.2 Place | 156 |
| | 4.3 People | 157 |
| | 4.4 Price | 157 |
| | 4.5 Promotions | 157 |
| 5. | The restaurant critic: Friend or foe? | 157 |
| 6. | Web opportunities | 158 |

**13 Cost Control** — 161

| | | |
|---|---|---|
| 1. | Keep control systems simple | 162 |
| 2. | Standard recipes | 164 |
| 3. | Standard purchase specifications | 167 |
| 4. | Supplier selection | 167 |
| 5. | Purchasing | 170 |
| 6. | Par stocks | 172 |
| 7. | Receiving | 173 |
| 8. | Storage | 174 |
| 9. | Perpetual inventories | 175 |
| 10. | Issuing | 177 |
| 11. | Service area control | 179 |
| 12. | Cash control | 180 |
| | 12.1 Cashing out | 182 |
| | 12.2 Daily sales reconciliation | 182 |
| | 12.3 Floats | 185 |

| | | |
|---|---|---|
| 13. | Till procedures | 185 |
| | 13.1 Pulling the till | 186 |
| | 13.2 Spotters | 186 |
| | 13.3 Skims | 187 |
| | 13.4 Counterfeit money | 187 |
| **14** | **Bars and Pubs** | **189** |
| 1. | Responsible service of alcohol | 190 |
| 2. | Handling difficult situations | 191 |
| 3. | Bar service and products | 193 |
| | 3.1 Bar service | 193 |
| | 3.2 Bar products | 194 |
| 4. | Bar equipment and small wares | 196 |
| | 4.1 Bar equipment | 196 |
| | 4.2 Small wares | 197 |
| | 4.3 Disposable goods | 198 |
| | 4.4 Bar condiments and juices | 199 |
| | 4.5 Garnishes | 199 |
| 5. | Glassware | 199 |
| 6. | Control Systems | 201 |
| | 6.1 Mechanical controls | 202 |
| 7. | Entertainment | 204 |
| 8. | Advertising and Promotion | 205 |
| | 8.1 Advertising | 205 |
| | 8.2 Promotional strategies | 206 |
| | 8.3 Public relations | 208 |
| **Conclusion** | | **211** |
| **Bibliography** | | **213** |

## Checklists

| | | |
|---|---|---|
| 1 | Business plan checklist | 27 |
| 2 | Market feasibility study checklist | 35 |
| 3 | POS system | 91 |
| 4 | Hiring/interview checklist | 107 |
| 5 | Orientation procedures | 109 |
| 6 | Floor training checklist | 110 |
| 7 | Analyze your readiness to start and run your restaurant or bar | 210 |

## Samples

| | | |
|---|---|---|
| 1 | Construction budget cost summary | 41 |
| 2 | Equipment list (Generic) | 43 |
| 3 | Income statement | 47 |
| 4 | Kitchen small wares | 96 |
| 5 | Job description | 103 |
| 6 | Job specifications | 104 |
| 7 | Job ad | 106 |
| 8 | Performance appraisal | 115 |
| 9 | Meeting agenda | 120 |
| 10 | Standard recipe | 166 |
| 11 | Food cost form | 168 |
| 12 | Purchase order | 171 |
| 13 | Inventory | 176 |
| 14 | Perpetual inventory/bin card | 178 |
| 15 | Server cash-out sheet | 183 |
| 16 | Bartender's summary | 184 |

## Worksheet

| | | |
|---|---|---|
| 1 | Competition analysis | 32 |

# Dedication

This work is dedicated to our co-author, Brian Cooper, whose untimely passing has deeply saddened us. He would have been pleased to see this work completed. He was a mentor, a colleague, and a friend. His intelligence, boundless energy, and lifelong passion and love for the hospitality industry have made it better place for all of us.

*— Brian Floody*
*— Gina McNeill*

# Acknowledgments

We gratefully acknowledge the contributions made by our editors, Catherine Bennett and Judy Phillips, at Self-Counsel Press. They have encouraged and supported us throughout this process. We'd also like to thank the many industry professionals and "F & Fs" (those wonderful friends and family members) who have lent us their encouragement, advice, and humor.

# *Introduction*

This "how to" book is a labor of love, created by three professional restaurateurs and pub owners, and based on a combined total of more than 100 years of personal experience in designing, owning, and running dozens of restaurants and pubs as well as instructing tens of thousands of college students and adults.

The conceptualization, establishment, and operation of a restaurant is a very personal experience built around a dream whose time has come. A restaurant, bar, or pub is a small retail business with a specialized product or service offered to a very localized target market. No doubt before you decided to investigate the potential for turning your dream into a reality, you looked at a concept that brought joy into your heart and visions of happiness — and, we hope, profit — into your life.

It is estimated that every year approximately one-third of all new restaurants or pubs go bankrupt or close, many from undercapitalization, some from failing to properly identify a concept that fits the owner's lifestyle. Most fail because the owner has become disenchanted with his or her concept, which had been altered as a result of persuasion by a moneylender or partner. You must remain true to your vision or you will be frustrated and gradually lose interest in achieving your goals.

Several years ago, a good friend of co-author Brian Cooper operated a successful small bakery he inherited from his parents. His was a rich life. He owned a cottage by a lovely lake where he spent most summer weekends, and he traveled the world together with his friends. One day, he was approached by the developers of a new mall with more than 100 retail stores. Having a bakery in this mall became his dream. The mall manager and his friends convinced him to add a considerable take-out menu to his bakery. His architect and his chef convinced him to add a sit-down restaurant and tavern that specialized in steaks, seafood, and — can you believe it — Chinese food. To accommodate this menu, his kitchen occupied 40 percent of the precious, high-rent floor space. Suddenly, weekends at the cottage were out, and his friends went on cruises without him while he managed a larger and larger staff. He became a slave to his new operation and lost interest in his original bakery. His chef left to open his own Chinese restaurant. Eventually Brian's friend had a heart attack and died. The business went bankrupt and was replaced with a very successful bagel and donut shop and a chain pizza house.

Everyone will be available and anxious to tell you how to design and operate your dream restaurant or pub. But will they be there to make your monthly payments at the bank? *Trust only in yourself.*

The expression of your restaurant, bar, or pub concept is your dream. Never deviate from your dream unless the alternative is fully acceptable to you.

By investing in this guide you are taking the first step toward realizing your goals. Our responsibility is to point out the challenges you may face and to suggest tips on how to avoid many of the mistakes we made in realizing our dreams. There is no one correct recipe for success in the food service and hospitality industry. Many of our friends claim that luck is crucial to success; however, we believe that any luck is a direct result of good solid business practices.

If after reading this guide you decide to continue on to design, build, and operate your restaurant, bar, or pub, we share in your delight. However, if we convince you to reconsider the viability of your dream before investing large sums of money and precious time in it, we will also have accomplished what we set out to do.

We will be focusing on the development of a mid-size, 60- to 150-seat, owner-operated, table-service restaurant. This type of restaurant may be described as family style, bistro, grill, or casual dining. We will guide you through the major steps in planning such a venture, but much of this information can be applied to other types of restaurants.

We will highlight certain important issues that can become turning points (or, as we call them, critical decision points) that we feel must be addressed before you continue your planning process. Take particular care over these.

Many of you who read this book will have little or no experience in building or operating a restaurant or pub. Others will have many years of experience in the front or back of the house and are looking only for a few tips on how to bring your dream to a profitable reality. Each chapter of this book is complete in itself as long as you keep in mind that whenever you radically change the focus of your operation, you must consider whether *you* are satisfied to operate under the new conditions that will result from altering your original concept.

Before you continue, attempt to visit as many similar operations as possible. Now is the only time you will have sufficient opportunity to view the mistakes made by your competitors. If possible, take on a full- or part-time position with a competitor and diary the strengths and weaknesses of his or her establishment and style of management. Join and participate in the trade associations that best serve your type of business and talk to the professionals. Attend a continuing education program at a nearby college or university to hone the skills that complement your knowledge; it will be time well spent before you begin to face those critical decision points and invest large amounts of capital and time.

In writing our book, we have established a sequence for starting and running a restaurant that made the most sense to us. We suggest you read it first from cover to cover as we present it, then go back to reread and underline any sections you feel you need to research or consider further.

To further assist you we have developed some concepts that may assist you in keeping things in perspective:

- ☞ *Critical decision points*: Those moments when you come to important crossroads and must decide if this exercise is indeed worth it. Continue on only if you can accept the risk you are taking.

- ☞ *Key points*: Ideas that we have tried and found useful.

- ☞ *Worksheets*: Work for you to do on your own to see if your numbers will add up to a successful venture. We will give examples of a variety of operations, but when you deal with your lending institution you will have to tailor this data to local conditions.

- ☞ *Checklists*: These are provided in several chapters to help you ensure that you have not forgotten anything critical to bringing your dream to a reality.

# Part 1
# EVALUATING YOUR DREAM

This part of the book describes a working path to take your dream of owning and operating a restaurant from concept to reality. At this point, you have been over the details in your mind and have discussed your vision with friends and family. Now you must be able to clearly define your goals and demonstrate them in writing in a manner that shows that you have carefully researched your concept and the marketplace. This narrative description of your dream is called the business plan. It becomes a tool that can help you and your potential investors evaluate the profitability of your proposed restaurant. This is a turning point, or a critical decision point as mentioned in the introduction: your decision to proceed with the formal business plan is the point at which you commit to outlining and writing down what has been only verbally discussed until now. It is a crucial step to take on the road to building your dream.

Chapters 1 and 2 touch on some points you should clarify before beginning your business plan. Chapter 3 begins with a brief overview of the business plan, then moves on to describe the feasibility study: the gathering of demographic information, the competition analysis, and the assessment of potential demand/revenue generators. Chapter 4 deals with the financial plan, details the financial statements required for your business plan, and concludes with a list of resources.

# Chapter 1
# BEFORE YOU START

Starting a restaurant involves many decisions. A prospective restaurateur must consider both the concept and the business aspect of his or her new venture. This chapter briefly highlights some important areas to think about before developing your plan for your new operation.

## 1. The Restaurateur as Entrepreneur and Entertainer

The successful restaurateur is a combination of entrepreneur (or businessperson) and entertainer (at times, even a magician). Your success depends on your ability to entertain your customer in your personalized theater. A restaurant or pub is simply a retail business that has been decorated and staffed to fit a specific production, as in a theater. Your menu is your script, your employees are your players, and your ability to balance finances determines the success or failure of your season. Predicting which of the latest trends will keep your customers coming back when there are so many restaurants competing for their time and money is theater at its best. Your customers act on a daily basis as your critics, and you are wise to listen carefully to their comments. Survey your customers while they are dining in your operation; often they will provide you with valuable tips on ways to improve your operation. You can trust plates returning from customer tables, and even the garbage can be an indicator of success or failure. If customers are dissatisfied with their meal and tell you, you have a chance to make corrections and keep them as patrons. Continue to operate without making changes and you run the risk not only of losing your loyal customers, but also of them telling their friends about their negative experience with your establishment.

## 2. The Menu

The menu is the most important document you will ever prepare. The following are only a few of the reasons your menu is crucial to your success:

- ☞ It describes your dream to your potential customers.
- ☞ It highly influences your location selection and marketing plan.
- ☞ It clearly influences your décor plan.
- ☞ It influences the design and layout of your kitchen and restaurant.
- ☞ It determines who your customers will be and influences your employee selection.
- ☞ It is a starting point for developing your pro forma income statement.

Everything, including your choice of partners and staff, is built around your choice of menu items.

If, for instance, your specialty will be the best Buffalo wings in town, your menu then necessitates a deep-fat fryer, an exhaust system, and a fire-extinguishing system in your kitchen. A casual décor usually complements such a menu, and your restaurant should be located near a family population base. Your employees' skill level will be less important than it would be if you have a more sophisticated menu. You will probably have a fast turnover of customers and a low check average. One simple decision influences a great deal of your dream.

**6**  *Start and run a restaurant business*

Before you look for partners to invest in your operation, prepare a draft menu for discussion. Place items on that menu only if they are within your personal capacity to prepare. Co-author Brian Cooper, in all his years of operating his own restaurants, only put items on a menu that in a pinch — or in a snowstorm or whenever his cook gave him an ultimatum — he could prepare himself until a replacement could be hired and trained.

(For more about menus, see chapter 10, "Your Menu.")

## 3. Trends

It is important for you to differentiate between trends and fads. At the time of writing this book, there has been a trend toward light and healthy foods and away from deep-fried foods and heavy sauces. These trends take years to develop, and some will become part of the food culture for decades. Many restaurants, however, have bucked these trends, to their great success. On the one hand, your ability to anticipate or initiate these trends will lead you to fame and fortune. Fads, on the other hand, are short term and disappear quickly once they saturate the market or when the public tires of them. The current fad of sandwich wraps in quick-service restaurants may or may not become a trend, depending on customer support. It is critical to recognize whether your new idea is a trendsetter or merely a fad that will come and go within a season.

The restaurant business is constantly looking for new ways to draw in customers, and is therefore always changing and evolving with the trends of the day. For example, today's customer would not be impressed with the "noveau cuisine" offerings of the 1980s. Fusion was the word in the 1990s, when we saw a strong Asian influence blending with North American or Californian cuisine. This decade took multiculturalism from the streets and neighborhoods to the table. This movement is still reflected in today's menu offerings, and customers are demanding true ethnic cuisines and indigenous ingredients. They are clamoring for authentic food that represents its country's fare and flavors. Malaysian, Vietnamese, and Taiwanese menus are growing more popular than before as this trend increases.

Another trend that continues to grow as our population ages is "heart smart" menu offerings. Health food is no longer an alternative cuisine, offered only in "veggie" restaurants. Customers are demanding menu choices that are not only delicious, but are also low in both saturated

*Before you start* **7**

fat and cholesterol and are healthy. Organic foods are now becoming mainstream as more people demand that food producers and those preparing foods act responsibly.

We have also seen a shift in where the food is prepared. The trend has been to take the kitchen out of the back of the house and bring it to center stage. Chefs are now celebrities, and the customer wants to be part of the action, often sitting at tables in full view of the kitchen. To be successful in this industry you will have to be continually prepared to grow, stay current with your clientele, and have fun!

# 4. *Types of Restaurants*

There are dozens of restaurant concepts from which you can choose in planning your dream. It is unlikely that any one concept will meet all the goals you have in mind, but try choosing the one from those mentioned below that most closely describes your operation and work with it throughout this guide. We have purposely limited the kinds of restaurants discussed here to a few general types, but with careful research, experience, and a lot of perspiration — and even some luck — you will develop a unique style of operation that fits your vision and strengths.

## 4.1 *The gourmet- or fine-dining room*

This restaurant is best described as a formal dining room, usually with tablecloths and linen napkins (hence the term "white-tablecloth operation," which is sometimes used to describe this sort of restaurant). These restaurants were often found in hotels, where the higher costs of operating can be absorbed into a larger operating budget. The prices tend to be high; the customer turnover, low.

The entire meal is a performance event that can take several hours. Location is not usually the key to the restaurant's success, since customers will often go out of their way to come to such a destination restaurant. Service is provided by a well-trained wait staff professional, who is skilled in building a high guest check. The wait staff are, in effect, commissioned salespeople paid a gratuity based on a percentage of the total bill presented at the end of the performance. The ability to merchandise that profitable appetizer, the second cocktail or bottle of fine wine, that sinfully rich dessert, specialty coffee, or after-dinner beverage will turn a fine meal into a profitable feast. The artistic features are provided by a well-known chef, who leaves his or her imprint

**8** *Start and run a restaurant business*

on the restaurant's menu. Care must be taken so that when your chef leaves, you don't lose your clientele to his or her new location.

We do not recommend that you choose a fine-dining concept for your first venture into the restaurant industry, unless you have had extensive hands-on experience, in both the front and back of the house, in several well-run fine-dining operations. In most cases these restaurants are chef driven, and the chef would have some ownership. Costs are very high. These establishments rely heavily on the business-expense-account and special-occasion diners, and a visit to such a restaurant often serves the customer as an evening's entertainment.

## 4.2 The family, mid-size, casual restaurant (also known as the bistro or grill)

These restaurants lend themselves to owner operation and will rely on the local population for support. There has been a growth in the number of this kind of restaurant, as people eat out more frequently due to longer working hours, dual-career families, and higher incomes. Providing food and service at a family restaurant doesn't require as much of a performance on the part of you and your staff as the fine-dining experience would, but you will want to get to know your customers personally and make them feel at home.

Family restaurants share characteristics with both the quick-service restaurant (discussed below) and the fine-dining restaurant (discussed above). You will need to design a menu that aids the customers in quickly making choices from a list of profitable items, assisted by a friendly and helpful server, who again is a commissioned salesperson. Usually you want to encourage adults to order alcoholic beverages and family members to order highly profitable desserts. At the same time, you do not want to make your guests so comfortable that they will stay so long as to prevent you from re-using the table for enthusiastic waiting guests.

Your challenge is to find ways to distinguish your concept from the similar operations in your marketplace. Here is where the design, ambiance, and quality of both food and service can be used to do just that. The owner's personality can be an important factor in making this difference.

*Before you start* **9**

### 4.3 The quick-service or fast-food restaurant

This style of restaurant usually features paper napkins and little or no service. The food is often purchased frozen and fully prepared so that the menu items can be quickly cooked and served. The skill level of the cooks will be minimal, and therefore the labor costs can be kept down. The average checks are much lower than in other types of restaurants, and revenue must be generated by high turnover. The style of service is minimal so that a fast turnover of customers will be possible. Most quick-service restaurants feature take-out and/or delivery.

Here, location is key to success. Locating even a donut or bagel shop on the wrong side of the street or highway can doom an otherwise excellent concept.

Specialization in a quick-service restaurant is important. You want to present a small, targeted menu that encourages customers to make up their minds, eat, and vacate the premises as quickly as possible, making way for new, eagerly waiting clients. Many fast-service restaurants fail because of the addition of unneeded and unprofitable items that are not compatible with the original concept.

### 4.4 Social and contract caterers

Although not dealt with specifically in this book, social and contract caterers are a major part of the restaurant industry. Whether located in a small or large hotel, a school, a hospital, or a retirement home, they form part of a fast-growing industry. Many family, quick-service, and fine-dining restaurants find that adding home, wedding, or business catering allows them finally to be profitable. In the slow periods between breakfast, lunch, and dinner, highly skilled and expensive employees are underused. Preparing for a large catering contract provides additional, much-needed revenue, and also provides management and staff with variety in their daily routine.

One of Brian Cooper's most successful restaurant friends had a business located in a large office tower. He found that catering to office parties and boardrooms became the most successful and profitable part of his business. Another friend found that preparing specialty (take-home) meals and featuring them in a local supermarket became so successful that a separate facility was needed to produce sufficient take-home items. In a situation like this one, however, you must always take care that the supermarket doesn't decide that it can open its own deli and cut you out.

# Chapter 2
# THE STRUCTURE OF YOUR BUSINESS

Before you proceed to developing your business plan as described in the next chapter, you should decide whether you wish to operate your restaurant as a sole proprietorship, a partnership, or a corporation. Each structure has distinct characteristics, so take care in deciding which one will serve you best. We strongly recommend that you consult your lawyer, accountant, and a financial planner for assistance in choosing. Below is a brief overview of each structure.

## 1. *The Sole Proprietorship*

By far the simplest of the business structures mentioned above is the sole proprietorship: a business owned and run by one person. As a sole proprietor you are responsible only to yourself and, of course, the financial institution with which you will be dealing.

## 1.1 Advantages

There are a number of advantages to operating your business as a sole proprietor:

- ☞ *Quick start.* You can begin doing business immediately as a sole proprietor. Documentation is minimal; all you really need to obtain is a business license, and no complicated partnership agreements need to be written.

- ☞ *Low cost.* Apart from obtaining a business license, no legal measures need be taken to set up as a sole proprietor; therefore, no legal fees are involved.

- ☞ *Possession of profits and assets.* All earnings and assets of the business are regarded as the personal income and personal property of the sole proprietor, and may be disposed of as the proprietor wishes.

- ☞ *Potential tax benefits.* As mentioned above, the earnings of the business are regarded as the personal income of the proprietor, and must be declared as such on all tax forms. However, should a sole proprietorship incur a loss, that loss can be used to decrease the proprietor's personal income tax.

- ☞ *Quick wind down or sale.* A business operated as a sole proprietorship can be closed or sold according to the proprietor's wishes. (Note, however, that legal responsibilities to employees and creditors must nonetheless be fulfilled.)

## 1.2 Disadvantages

Some disadvantages of operating as a sole proprietor include the following:

- ☞ *Possession of debts.* Any debts incurred by the business are regarded as the personal debts of the sole proprietor.

- ☞ *Liability.* As a sole proprietor, your liability for the debts and obligations of your business is unlimited. Furthermore, an unsatisfied business creditor can resort to your personal assets if you cannot pay your business debts.

- ☞ *Potential tax problems.* A sole proprietorship is not eligible for certain tax breaks available to corporations. This is likely to become an issue as your restaurant becomes more and more profitable.

☞ *Limited financing options.* Banks and other lending in
may be less enthusiastic about providing loans to sole p
than to partnerships and corporations. You will be re
put up personal assets worth almost equal to the val
loan, as well as personally guarantee any amount bor

Due to the volatility of the restaurant industry, it is difficu
erate a restaurant as a sole proprietorship unless you have a
heritance or have recently won a lottery. Nonetheless, once y
prepared your financial plan (see chapter 4, "The Business Plan;
nancial Plan") and carefully researched your personal capacity
ate without partners, you may be able to operate at least at the start as
a sole proprietor. We highly recommend it.

Often, individuals believe that franchise opportunities are similar to
sole proprietorships. However, as you will see in section **4.**, they can be
looked on more truly as a partnership, with all the challenges that go
along with that business structure.

# 2. The Partnership

A partnership is an intermediate form of business organization, more
complex than an individual proprietorship but less complex than a limited company. It is simply an agreement between two or more parties to
conduct a business for profit.

## 2.1 Advantages

There are many advantages to operating your business as a partnership:

☞ *Quick start.* As in the case of the sole proprietorship, in a partnership, you and your partners can start doing business immediately. However, you must register your partnership's name. It
is also advisable for all partners to enter into a written partnership agreement.

☞ *Pooling of resources.* Your restaurant venture will be strengthened
by the combined skills and financial resources of several people, rather than only what you alone can bring to the business.

☞ *Possession of profits.* Profits earned by the business flow directly
to the partners, according to the distribution formula to which
the partners agreed in their partnership agreement. Each partner declares this income personally.

*The structure of your business* **13**

> ☞ *Potential tax benefits.* Any losses incurred by the partnership can be used to decrease the personal income tax of the partners.

## 2.2 **Disadvantages**

There are, however, some disadvantages to a partnership:

> ☞ *Possession of debts.* Each partner is responsible, both individually and together with the other partners, for debts incurred by the partnership.

> ☞ *Liability.* Each partner is personally liable for the debts and obligations of the partnership, and this liability is unlimited. The personal assets of the partners may be attached to satisfy the business's debts.

> ☞ *Potential tax problems.* A partnership is not eligible for certain tax breaks available to corporations, and all partners will be taxed at the individual rate. This is likely to become an issue as your restaurant becomes more and more profitable.

> ☞ *Personality conflicts.* The more people involved in the partnership, the greater the potential for disagreement.

> ☞ *Instability.* A partnership dissolves upon the death or withdrawal of any partner or upon the acceptance of a new partner. In each case, a new partnership agreement will have to be drawn up to allow the partnership to carry on.

Most new restaurants begin as partnerships. Each partner brings a unique quality to the business. One may be the financial or business specialist, another may have years of experience in running a similar restaurant. More and more we find financial, accounting, and public-relations specialists teaming up with a kitchen manager or chef. Each partner should bring talent or capital to the business.

If you will be operating your restaurant in partnership with other people, it is crucial that you create a written partnership agreement, and we advise you to do this with the aid of an independent lawyer (one who is not affiliated with any of the partners). If you follow only this advice, your investment in this book will be repaid many times over. A partnership agreement will cover, among other things, the partners' rights, responsibilities, contributions, and liabilities, as well as procedures for voting, dispute resolution, buying/selling of shares among the partners, and termination of the partnership. You may wish to use the *Partnership Agreement* forms on CD available from Self-Counsel Press.

Most partnerships, unless carefully structured, end in failure. The operating partner spends countless hours running the restaurant, with little initial financial reward. Financial-investment partners never seem to receive expected returns quickly enough, and often lose interest in the business (with which they have little day-to-day involvement) and want to divert their money into another "more successful" venture. Initial interests wane, and lives and priorities change. Often no one is to blame for a partnership turned sour, but the best time to consider the potential breakup is at the beginning, before the signatures go on any business loan.

A partnership agreement, signed by all the partners, will set specific terms by which a partnership can be amicably ended. Often, the ending of a partnership is triggered by one or more partners expressing a desire to dissolve the partnership and settling a price for the original and earned revenue accomplished as a result of the partnership. Rarely do partners agree on the current value of the business at time of dissolution. A simple but effective clause can be inserted in the buy/sell provisions that requires that one partner tender to purchase the assets of the other partner or partners. If the partners who are being tendered upon are not satisfied, they can themselves take over the business by offering $1.00 more to the tendering partner. This clause prevents any partner from bidding "cheap" for the business, and allows both sides to walk away from the investment with reasonable satisfaction. However, you must set the buy/sell terms before the partnership is formalized.

Go into any partnership with your eyes wide open. Say to yourself at every stage, "What *could* go wrong with my partnership?" and realize that at some time during the partnership, something probably *will* go wrong with it. Doing your homework now can prevent the lawyers from getting rich at your expense later.

## 3. The Corporation

A corporation is a legal entity in and of itself, and exists separately from its shareholders. Often a corporate structure will evolve out of a partnership, once you and those involved can more clearly see the potential of your restaurant.

### 3.1 Advantages

Some advantages of a corporation include the following:

- ☞ *Limited liability.* No member of a company is personally liable for the debts, obligations, or acts of the company over and above the amount paid or owed for the purchase of shares, unless he or she has signed a personal guarantee.

- ☞ *Potential tax benefits.* Corporations have access to certain tax benefits that are not available to proprietorships or partnerships.

- ☞ *Ease of financing.* Because of the limited liability mentioned above, many investors feel more secure about putting money into a corporation, knowing that their personal assets are protected.

- ☞ *Stability.* Because a corporation is an entity separate from its shareholders, it does not cease to exist upon the death of a shareholder. In addition, shares can be transferred without disturbing the management of the business.

### 3.2 Disadvantages

Some disadvantages of a corporation include the following:

- ☞ *Expense.* There are substantial costs involved in incorporating.

- ☞ *Potential tax difficulties.* Operation losses and tax credits must remain within the corporation and cannot be used by individual shareholders against personal tax.

- ☞ *Difficulty of dissolution.* Because a corporation is a legal entity, it can be difficult to dissolve. All the obligations of the corporation must be satisfied and documentation must be filed with the appropriate government authorities.

Depending on the terms contained in the shareholder's agreement you can easily expand your dream operation and franchise additional units as time and finances permit. If one investor disagrees with the direction of new growth, the will of the majority of investors will prevail, allowing for smoother operation. Again, as with partnerships, we strongly recommend that you enlist the aid of a lawyer in drawing up a shareholder's agreement, including a buy/sell provision.

# 4. Franchising

Franchising is the leasing of a name, concept, and management system for a percentage of sales. Many people consider franchising an easier and less risky means by which to enter an arena as fraught with pitfalls as the restaurant business. And indeed, in some ways it is. New franchisees, especially in national or international companies, do have a much higher success rate on average than independent, first-time restaurateurs.

We will touch on franchises here only insomuch as they fail to meet one of the fundamental premises of this book: a franchise, no matter how successful or financially viable, is not your dream; it is someone else's dream! Franchising is an excellent method for the franchisor to expand his or her dream using other people's (new franchisees') capital. But as a franchisee, you will pay, by way of royalties and other fees, to help the growth of someone else's dream, long after you have become a seasoned restaurateur with little more to learn from your franchisor "partner."

This is not to say that a franchise, especially with a nationally known company, is not an excellent business opportunity. Many franchisees are happy with their corporate partners and line up to open new units (which are usually quite expensive). Franchises work best at the fast-food end of the food-service continuum. Fast-food franchise restaurants are selling sameness. The customer knows what to expect, and chooses to go to a McDonald's, for example, because it will be just like the last McDonald's he or she went to. And that is precisely why very little leeway is allowed in franchises for the creative ideas of the individual franchisee. In our experience, the dream of most new restaurant entrepreneurs is to establish their own concepts to reflect their own personalities and what they think they have to offer the public. The very elements that make your restaurant unique are often at odds with the basic franchise precept: the duplication of someone else's already-developed dream. We have found that the people who are attracted to the idea of opening their own restaurant usually find the tightly controlled climate of the franchise experience too restrictive, and often, after a few years they want to break out on their own.

If you do opt for franchising, however, there are several things you would do well to keep in mind. Carefully check out the particular franchise that interests you. Try to find answers to as many of these questions as you can:

- How well known is the franchise in which you are interested? (Remember, you will be paying a substantial amount of money, in part because the product you will be selling is supposed to have a certain amount of market penetration already established by the franchisor. If it doesn't, what exactly are you paying for?)
- How long has the franchise operation been operating?
- Is it financially stable?
- Are new locations being opened regularly?
- Have locations failed? If so, why?
- Contact other franchisees. Do they have complaints?
- Is your proposed territory clearly defined? Do you have guaranteed exclusivity?
- Can you select your own location?
- Are there standards to be met for the location? How flexible are they?
- Are the various kinds of equipment and fixtures specified? Must you purchase them from the franchisor?
- Are there training programs in place for you and your staff? Who pays for these? You or the franchisor?
- Are the prices set? Are you allowed to offer sales incentives in your store alone if business becomes sluggish?
- Is there a minimum amount of product that must be purchased from the franchisor?
- How much input do you have in franchise-wide advertising campaigns?
- Does the franchisor have bank-financing programs available for you?

Some other questions about the franchise agreement itself you should consider are:

- What is the duration of the agreement?

**18** *Start and run a restaurant business*

☞ Under what conditions can the agreement be terminated?

☞ Can you resell the franchise? What conditions apply?

☞ What happens if you die? Will your heirs be allowed to continue the business?

For more information on business structures, see *Canadian Legal Guide for Small Business,* a title in the Self-Counsel Legal Series.

**KEY POINT**

The key to all these questions and many others is the franchise agreement itself. If ever there is an important time to get good legal advice, it is before you sign probably one of the most important (and usually the longest) legal contract of your life. Take the contract to a well-recommended lawyer who has experience in restaurant franchises. The advice of a lawyer with very specific knowledge and experience in this specialized area is worth a sometimes exorbitant fee for a few hours' time.

These questions and others, especially regarding bankruptcy or the agreement's termination, renewal, transfer, or sale, are critical decision points when considering the purchase of any franchise.

For further information, contact:

The American Franchisee Association
Phone: 312-431-0545
www.infonews.com/afa

Canadian Franchise Association
Phone: 905-625-2896
www.cfa.ca

There are any number of franchise information Web sites. Try:

Franchise Info Mall
Phone: 1-877-Info-Mall
www.franchiseinfomall.com

Or speak with the franchising section of most Canadian Banks. The Business Development Bank of Canada also has general franchising information:

> Phone: 1-877-232-2269
> www.bdc.ca

## 5. *Building Your Team*

It's important that you invest valuable time in choosing your business structure and partners. Harmony will prevail only if each member has a role or purpose. Choose your partners or investors based on what they can bring to the group. If one member is expert at running the kitchen (often known as "the back of the house," and sometimes as "the heart of the house"), that person should participate as an expert in developing and training the employees under his or her direction. You will also need someone to specialize in running the "front of the house" — that part of your establishment that is visible to your customers. This person would be responsible for the service standards, and for developing a personality or feel for the area outside the kitchen. Usually, in a small restaurant, this would be one of the owners (possibly you).

The front of the house and the back of the house must work together to create the harmony and balance of the food, wine, and ambiance in the restaurant. The front-of-the-house person must have a finger on the pulse or heartbeat of the operation. He or she should be adept at training and developing the service staff, including wait staff and bartenders. Wine is becoming important to complete a dining experience. If you intend to feature a wine menu in your restaurant, the front-of-the-house person should be willing to expand his or her knowledge in this area. The chef and the front-of-the-house person should be able to suggest particular wines to complement the menu items and, in turn, the wait staff can be trained to do the same.

Similarly, one member of your team should deal with the investment and/or legal side of the business. The "numbers" person must communicate with the other partners at all times so the project remains financially viable. Regular meetings should be held to ensure that all parties work together.

The team should be on board early in the planning stage. Complement your abilities by hiring professionals who are strong in areas where you are weak. Often the partners do not bring a chef or kitchen manager on board early enough to prevent major design errors. Once you have drafted your menu, it is time to hire that kitchen manager/chef to help design your kitchen (and to begin putting his or her imprint on the menu). Not allowing for an essential piece of kitchen equipment can create major problems and expense later on. Building an oversized kitchen can cost you floor space that otherwise could be used to seat customers.

Another reason for putting your team together early is so that when you go to lending institutions for financing, your loan application will be supported by your choice of partners or team members. You will be able to profile their successes and their competencies in the field, which, together with your business plan, should help convince the lenders that you are a "good risk."

The downside of putting the team together early is that they may not be available when the actual restaurant opens unless you are prepared to offer them a share of the business. If they don't have a vested interest in the project, it may be hard for you to sustain their enthusiasm, given the time between conception of your restaurant and its actual opening. In addition, few people can afford to go without a salary during this period. However, the lenders will want some assurances that the team you present in the application for your loan will actually be there when you open!

# Chapter 3
# THE BUSINESS PLAN: FEASIBILITY STUDY

## 1. The Business Plan: An overview

The business plan is a formal written presentation of your restaurant concept. It is used to introduce your business to potential lenders and should contain enough information for the reader (the investor) to judge the venture's potential profitability. A business plan is a requirement if you are seeking a loan from financial institutions or trying to get "F&F" (family and friends) funds. It is also the blueprint of your business dream and will serve as a guide during your business's lifetime.

A well-researched and properly documented plan is a prerequisite to a successful business and should be professionally presented. You can gather the material yourself and have it spiral bound at a print store, or you can hire a consulting firm that specializes in the hospitality industry to conduct the feasibility study for you and then assist you in writing the business plan. Depending on your writing experience and financial-planning and research background — as well as your time limitations — it may be worthwhile to contract out this work. Whatever you choose, the plan must portray your ideas and passions and must communicate these to the lenders. If this is your first time approaching a lender for a small-business loan, it often helps to have the name of a reputable accounting or consulting firm attached to your proposal. They may already have established relationships with banks, which may help convince the lender of your ability to meet the loan obligations. Bankers are not experts in the hospitality field, but they are very aware of the high restaurant-fatality rate, and therefore often look to "experts" for their approval of a particular plan.

The essential parts of the business plan are as follows:

(a) *Cover page and index.*

(b) *Statement of objective.* If you are seeking money, state how much you need and other pertinent details.

(c) *Executive summary.* This is a brief synopsis of the company or partnership, and a description of the proposed restaurant, including:

    (i)   Its name, address, phone number, and Web site address, and any graphics that have been developed (i.e., logo or signage designs).

    (ii)  A description of the type and style of your proposed restaurant (e.g., fine dining, bistro, pub, casual dining). Summarize the overall concept as well as the kind of food, decor, and service style. A menu can be inserted here as well as an artist's rendering of the dining room, color scheme, and description of furniture and fixtures as they support your concept.

    (iii) Location. Describe the proposed site and why it was selected, as well as its access to major routes and other demand generators.

    (iv) Customer profile and target market. Describe the demographic characteristics of your customers. (You can use information from the feasibility study in section **2.** for this.)

    (v)  Your competition. Describe your competition, then focus on what makes your restaurant unique and how it will fill a void in the marketplace. Discuss how you will compete with existing restaurants. (Once again, the research you do for your feasibility study will be used here.)

(vi) Marketing and advertising strategies. Include any promotional material you've developed.

(vii) Historical information on the business, if applicable.

(viii) Management team. Describe the experience, expertise, and ability of the team members (chef, dining-room manager, wine steward, and restaurant designer) and emphasize their achievements in the industry. Include information on successes the members of your team have had in running similar restaurants.

(ix) Ownership and business structure. Describe who will own what percentage of your enterprise, and indicate the business structure (see chapter 2) under which you plan to operate.

(d) *Financial projections and documents.* These statements include your capital budget, projected income (or profit-and-loss) statement, your break-even analysis, projected balance sheet, and projected cash-flow analysis. (See chapter 4 for a further description of financial statements.) These statements should be created by an outside accountant, bookkeeper, or CPA. Also include a summary of your financial needs: indicate why you are applying for a loan, how much is needed, how much your own investment in the restaurant will be, and any other sources of funding. Describe how the funds will be used, and include any back-up information regarding costs of equipment and furnishings.

(e) *Supporting material to strengthen parts of your business plan.* This should include any information you can supply that outlines your previous success or achievements, such as:

(i) Résumés and personal letters from noteworthy industry associates or leaders recommending you as a professional and good "risk," as well as press clippings, editorials, testimonials, or awards that have been received by members of your team for outstanding achievement in the hospitality industry.

(ii) Copies of leases and agreements between you and landlords or equipment companies.

*The business plan: Feasibility study* **25**

(iii) Credit reports from banks and any established credit from suppliers or wholesalers.

Make copies of your business plan for yourself and each lender you approach. Having the business plan spiral bound will give it a professional look and reflect your intent to create a profitable business. Keep track of who has copies of your business plan.

When it comes to acquiring your financing, be sure to allow enough lead time. It may take up to six months after your business plan has been presented to actually receive the funds.

For more information on business plans, see *Preparing a Successful Business Plan*, another title in the Self-Counsel Business Series. You may also wish to use Checklist 1, "Business Plan Checklist," as a reference when pulling your business plan together.

## 2. The Feasibility Study

The feasibility study is an examination of your proposed restaurant in relation to the existing marketplace. It focuses on defining your competition as well as your potential customers in your selected location. It is called a "feasibility study" because it involves researching the viability of your operation in terms of competition and demand.

The feasibility study is comprised of an evaluation of both the supply of and the demand for your specific operation. There are firms that specialize in doing the research, compiling the data, and analyzing the results for you, but contracting out your feasibility study can be expensive. Nonetheless, after considering your knowledge of the industry and your time available to do the fieldwork, you may consider it worthwhile to hire a consultant. One internationally respected consulting firm specializing in the hospitality industry is Horwath Consultants, which has more than 250 offices in 80 countries around the world. There are also smaller independent consultants who specialize in the restaurant and hospitality industry who can provide a valuable service to you in the initial stages of your restaurant's development. Horwath's chairman, John Burt, has said that only a fraction of his company's business is restaurant related, as too few prospective restaurateurs do a feasibility study — that may be why so many restaurants fail! With a bankruptcy rate more than double that for the overall economy, it is vital that restaurateurs thoroughly research every aspect of their new venture.

**26**  *Start and run a restaurant business*

## *Checklist 1*
## BUSINESS PLAN CHECKLIST

**Check off the following items as you complete them.**

❏ Cover page

❏ Company name, address, telephone and fax numbers, e-mail address, and Web address or URL if applicable

❏ Key company contacts and their titles

❏ Table of contents

❏ Company summary (one-page synopsis of your company's aims and objectives, and the financing required)

❏ Company history and background, including responsibilities, qualifications, and short biographies of all principals and key personnel

❏ Details of your restaurant's style and market

❏ Proposed menu and ad copy

❏ Logo and artwork

❏ Feasibility studies and marketing research conducted

❏ Financial information

  ❏ summary of start-up costs

  ❏ loan required and collateral

  ❏ balance sheet

  ❏ revenue forecasts and projected income statement

  ❏ cash-flow statement

❏ Summary and appendices

These are the key components of the feasibility study:

☞ Target area analysis

☞ Population profile

☞ Economic profile

☞ Competition analysis

☞ Industry and tourism profile

☞ Cultural and recreation attractions

☞ Real estate marketplace

## 2.1  *Target area analysis*

The goal of your feasibility study is to assess the local competition and begin to understand your marketplace in terms of its demographics. To do this, you must first establish the boundaries of the area in which you wish to locate your restaurant. The area under consideration should then be described and mapped in terms of access via private vehicle using major highways and routes, public transit, and rail. Research the major communities located within the target area so that you can provide background descriptions on them in your feasibility study, giving emphasis to sectors of those communities that will affect demand for your services. History of the economic development in your target area can be obtained from municipal or town economic development offices. If you are not native to the area, this part of your study will be very valuable in helping you to understand your marketplace. Future development in the target area should be considered here: try to imagine how any new developments will affect your restaurant.

## 2.2  *Population profile*

Understanding "who" your customers are and "where" they will be coming from is one of the challenges facing a new operation. If you are a neighborhood establishment drawing on the local community, this challenge is the starting point for developing a profile of your customers.

One place to begin your research is with census data for your target area. The Bureau of the Census (a division of the United States Department of Commerce, phone 301-457-4608, or on the Web at <www.census.gov/>) is the primary source of population and demographic information in the United States. The US Census of Population and

Housing is conducted every ten years. To obtain more current information, you can contact a demographic-research firm for estimates based on computer-generated projections. Local sources, including municipal planning departments, zoning departments, and building inspectors, are also excellent sources for information on your target area. The World Wide Web is another place to begin your search for information. Many communities have their economic development offices linked to their city's Web site, so you can start your information gathering from your office or home before heading out to do the field work.

In Canada, census information is taken every five years; this information is available from Statistics Canada (Statscan). You can phone them at 1-800-263-1136, or visit them on the Web at <www.statcan.ca>. The Financial Post Data Group (phone 1-800-661-7678, or on the Web at <www.financialpost.com>) is another source of detailed demographic information for the Canadian marketplace. They annually publish — in print and on CD-ROM — *Financial Post Markets: Canadian Demographics,* which contains demographic information on 700 Canadian markets, broken down by province, city, town, and census division, including data on education levels, labor force, consumer groups, income levels, population projections to 2002 and 2005, and a complete list of industrial development contacts. Copies are also available on loan from The Canadian Restaurant and Food Service Association library in Toronto (phone 416-923-8416, toll free at 1-800-387-5649, or on the Web at <www.crfa.ca>), or by purchase through the Financial Post Data Group.

The population of your target area should be reviewed in terms of its historical growth as well as its projected growth through the next ten-year period. The population by age group should be evaluated with respect to the community's ability to retain its younger segment to further the economic growth and development of the area. This information will also provide you with a sense of where your marketplace is headed and will help you determine whether your restaurant concept fits with the target area's population base.

Some other information that can be derived from the census data that will be valuable in establishing a community profile includes:

☞ Number of dwelling units by structure type

☞ Number of people that own versus rent their dwellings

☞ Average level of education of people in your target area, as well as their employment classifications

☞ Marital status/families by type

☞ Average household income

☞ Ethnic origin and percentage of population by languages spoken

☞ Percentage of population by age group

This information can assist you in putting together an accurate profile of your target customer and can be used to determine the fit or level of acceptance with which your concept will be met. Information on the languages spoken will also be valuable in determining the ethnic mix and diversity in your area. You can supplement the raw data gathered from census information and from city or town planning departments by "people watching" at establishments in your target area. Visiting the competition is a very good way of getting a firsthand look at your prospective clientele!

Information gathered from bartenders, wait staff, and restaurant managers can be invaluable and well worth the effort.

**H**ere is a story from co-author Gina McNeill — a story that demonstrates that not doing your demographics homework is a BIG mistake!

Murphy's White Horse Café was located in Egg Harbor, New Jersey, on the major route leading to Atlantic City from Philadelphia. The restaurant had been a local "gin mill," selling beer by the glass for less than 50 cents, and had no atmosphere to speak of — except for a beautiful, 3-feet-deep by 15-feet-long, solid-wood shuffleboard game. The Murphys purchased the tavern with hopes and dreams of turning it into a New York City–style operation. They were not counting on the locals to support the "new and improved" bar and restaurant, but instead were relying on the droves of people driving down the highway to the gambling dens in Atlantic City to stop in. Wrong! The cars headed directly to the blackjack tables at the casinos, and on the return trip their occupants were too broke to stop or had enjoyed the freebies at the casinos. The wooden shuffleboard was made into beautiful bar tables, much to the dismay of the locals, who, despite everything, came to be the backbone of the bar crowd!

## 2.3 Economic profile

Analysis of the retail and industrial strength of the community will help to determine if your proposed site is viable. "Location, location, location," more than anything else, is why an operation succeeds or fails. A location-related error is a permanent one, and every effort to analyze and understand site selection is critical. See chapter 6, "Choosing Your Restaurant's Location," for more information on location.

The economic profile should look at the growth or potential for growth within your target area. Determining the economic profile for the community can help you gauge the appropriateness of your type of restaurant for the area. This information can be gathered from economic development officers and city planners. A description of the mix of commercial, industrial, and retail businesses in the target area should be included in this part of the study. This information, along with the competition analysis, will help determine the positioning of your type of operation within the community.

## 2.4 Competition analysis

Any feasibility study must include an analysis of the competition in your target area. This may help you determine if there is a niche in the area that your type of restaurant can fill. Some restaurants in the target area may be designed on concepts that are similar to yours, and others maybe quite different. Spend some time in the target area and visit your competition. The town economic and development or business improvement office can provide a listing of local businesses. (You will also want to go to the town or city hall to see if there are any outstanding building permits for new construction of restaurants in the area.) You can use Worksheet 1, "Competition Analysis," to record the information you gather on your competition. This should be part of your feasibility study, and can be updated from time to time after your restaurant is established.

If you discover that there are other restaurants already in the area similar to the one you plan to operate, you must consider modifying your concept to better suit a vacant niche or think about opening in another location altogether. However, you may actually benefit from your competition generating a restaurant district (or "restaurant row" as it is known in the industry). People will often travel to a restaurant row knowing that they will have a greater selection of restaurants from which to choose. All the people and activity in a destination such as this

*The business plan: Feasibility study* **31**

# Worksheet 1
# COMPETITION ANALYSIS

| Restaurant name | | | | |
|---|---|---|---|---|
| Location | | | | |
| Type* | | | | |
| No. of seats | | | | |
| No. of staff | | | | |
| Meals served (B/L/D) | | | | |
| Average check | | | | |
| Ownership** | | | | |
| Customer age | | | | |
| Promotions or events | | | | |
| Significant features | | | | |

*Type: fine dining (FD), take out/limited seating (TO/LS), family style (FS), hotel restaurant (HR), bistro/pub (BP), ethnic (ETH), fast food (FF)

**Ownership: owner operated (OO), chef owned (CO), franchise/chain (F/C) generate a "buzz," which enhances the total entertainment/dining experience. However, the population base must be able to support the number and variety of restaurants, and there must be other demand generators nearby. Often these "rows" spring up close to supporting venues, such as the live-theater district in cities such as New York and Toronto, or near the waterfront, as in San Francisco's wharf area. Many towns and cities have cultivated a tourist hub centering around a significant feature of that area, and restaurants are part of the draw. If you are thinking of locating your restaurant in a restaurant row, visit your potential competition to find out how busy they are.

## 2.5 Industry and tourism profile

Research and then summarize the local industries in your target marketplace and emphasize their potential to generate business in your area. You can learn about them from the local chamber of commerce, Lions Club, Rotary Club, or other service clubs in the community. Once you have opened your restaurant, you may want to join one of these organizations; with luck, you will be hosting some of their luncheon meetings. Forging good relations and networking with the local business community is a prudent thing to do. Your restaurant may be able to provide lunches for management meetings, as well as dinners and special events sponsored by these companies.

The positive effects of tourism in your area and how it can benefit your operation should also be summarized in your study. Talking with other operators will give you a handle on how and when the tourist season influences their business. Information can also be gathered from your tourist and convention bureau or local business association. If you are going to focus on attracting the tourists, you should formulate a plan and make contacts with the bus companies or tour companies that do business in your area. Highlight the tourist segment in your marketing strategies, and include this potential revenue in your financial projections.

## 2.6 Cultural, recreational, and sporting events

Cultural, recreational, and sporting events can attract potential customers for your restaurant and should be researched when you prepare your feasibility study. Such events are known as demand generators, as they help increase the demand for food and beverages in the marketplace during specific times. If there is a town or city convention bureau or center for cultural affairs in your target area, you will be able to get information regarding numbers of people who have attended events in the past and will also be able to obtain estimates for future events.

## 2.7 The real estate marketplace

Important information can be learned from the local real estate office. They will be able to inform you of property values, home-building starts, and significant changes in the housing prices, and can give you an idea of what may be driving the marketplace. Again, your goal is to get a clear picture of your target area and begin to understand your potential customers. Commercial brokers will be able to provide information about recent business opportunities and sales in the area as well.

Checklist 2, "Market Feasibility Study Checklist," has been designed to help you stay on track with your research.

# 3. Pre-Opening Marketing Strategy

Once you have identified your target area and your potential customer base, your next challenge will be to create a plan to let potential customers know about your new restaurant. This will form an essential part of your business plan, and will be part of developing your marketing strategy and putting together an advertising and promotions budget.

The focus and objective in this early stage will be to find ways to "get the word out" and tell your story — generate a buzz about the new place in town, and create hype and anticipation about your opening. You must have clearly defined your customer base in your feasibility study as this is the groundwork you will use to select methods for reaching customers. Here are some means by which you can spread the news:

- ☞ Grand Opening "invitations" — a direct-mail piece to your target audience
- ☞ Flyers to be distributed within your target area
- ☞ Radio spots on selected stations, appealing to your potential customers
- ☞ Ad with coupon incentive in local newspapers
- ☞ Banner/signage in the window — a "dress the window" countdown to opening date

**34**   *Start and run a restaurant business*

## *Checklist 2*
## MARKET FEASIBILITY STUDY CHECKLIST

|  | Yes | No |
|---|---|---|
| **Target area analysis** | | |
| Visited the area, day and evening | ❑ | ❑ |
| Created map of the boundaries with access from major roadways | ❑ | ❑ |
| Identified key demand generators | ❑ | ❑ |
| **Analysis of the competition** | | |
| Visited the major competition and observed their operations | ❑ | ❑ |
| Completed worksheets on the major competitors | ❑ | ❑ |
| Visited business development/planning board office to determine if any new competition entering the marketplace | ❑ | ❑ |
| **Population and economic profile** | | |
| Gathered and analyzed population statistics | ❑ | ❑ |
| Determined that concept "fits" the population profile | ❑ | ❑ |
| Visited tourism office to determine the impact of convention and tourism on business | ❑ | ❑ |
| Created a description of the mix of commercial, industrial, and retail business | ❑ | ❑ |
| **Real estate marketplace** | | |
| Obtained the most recent sales/lease figures for comparable transactions in area | ❑ | ❑ |
| Determined what is driving commercial real estate in area | ❑ | ❑ |
| **Other** | | |
| Identified where outside help is necessary to complete checklist | ❑ | ❑ |

**Date completed** _____

☞ Media attention: Use a well-written press release to tip off local food writers about some unique aspect of your restaurant, such as your creative menu or talented chef.

☞ Internet banner ad and link placed on your town or city's Web site or your local newspaper's site. Explore Web sites of related food and beverage businesses and advertise on their sites. Try restaurant supply companies, food and beverage vendors, professional chefs' associations, restaurant news sites, local community colleges, and convention bureaus.

☞ Invitations to potential customers in your target area to participate in "focus groups" by way of a menu tasting or sampling

☞ A "joint" special promotion with one of your beer, wine, or spirit suppliers

☞ Announcement in the local business association or economic development publication

Your sales team in a restaurant is your service staff — word of mouth in the industry spreads quickly, so rely on them to pump up the opening.

We recommend that you marshal all your ideas and then find an advertising or marketing professional to help you with the final presentation of your ideas. Such professionals can help you create the look of your ads or promotional pieces so that they reflect your restaurant's concept and project a professional image. A graphic artist can assist you in developing a logo — a unifying image or graphic that can be used on all your communication pieces, including your business cards, letterhead, menu, and advertisements.

This marketing information can be used in your business plan to show potential investors that you have a plan for introducing your concept. Chapter 12, "Marketing," will focus on your ongoing marketing strategies once you have opened your restaurant.

**36**   *Start and run a restaurant business*

# Chapter 4
# THE BUSINESS PLAN: THE FINANCIAL PLAN

The financial plan is a crucial part of your business plan. There are two important reasons to create one. The first is simply for your own benefit. A carefully constructed financial plan will tell you whether your dream is financially viable. This is one of those critical decision points we mentioned earlier. If, after careful analysis, your financial projections tell you that you will not be able to achieve the profit necessary to make the project worthwhile, you must seriously consider making substantial modifications to your dream or even abandoning the project altogether. However, the second reason for creating a financial plan is that if it can demonstrate the profitability of the project, it can become a very valuable tool in convincing investors to back you.

A financial plan has several parts, but there are two major elements: a capital budget and a projected income statement. In other words, you need to show how much money you will require to get your restaurant up and running, and then show how the business will generate enough revenue to ensure you can repay your investment debts without difficulty. A financial plan usually consists of these segments:

- ☞ Capital budget
- ☞ Investment plan
- ☞ Projected income statement
- ☞ Break-even analysis
- ☞ Pro forma balance sheet
- ☞ Cash-flow analysis

# 1. The Capital Budget

Your capital budget details your start-up costs in several schedules or summaries. This will take some time and energy to research. Start-up costs are usually broken down into "hard" costs, such as the cost of building materials or equipment, and the more intangible "soft" costs, such as costs for designers, consulting advice, or training.

## 1.1 Hard costs

Common hard costs found in the capital budget of most new restaurants would be the following:

- ☞ The restaurant space itself (purchase price or lease)
- ☞ Renovation
- ☞ Equipment
- ☞ Furnishings
- ☞ Small wares
- ☞ Opening inventory

### 1.1a The restaurant space itself

Often the largest single cost in opening a restaurant is the purchase of either a free-standing building for the business or the lease of a premises.

#### Buy versus rent

The decision to purchase or lease your restaurant depends on many factors, not the least of which is your available financing. In most cases, a freestanding restaurant building is beyond the means of a single new

**38**   *Start and run a restaurant business*

entrepreneur. The debt incurred to purchase a building, even if the money is available, is often more than a small- or mid-size restaurant can support. Ordinarily, unless you have established a line of credit, the bank will want you to put up at least 20 percent (and usually more) of the total money needed. The lack of proper financing and working capital often results in a restaurant's failure to thrive. No one can completely determine the exact failure rate in this industry, because so many restaurants merely "fade away": owners cut their losses and sell just to get out of a downward spiral. However, if you are able to secure the financing needed, one advantage of purchasing is that you will own a tangible asset and you will have more control over the premises. Such ownership is usually a long-term investment.

There is an alternative to buying, though. Rather than borrow the money to buy the land and the building, many new restaurateurs choose to lease the space, and then get a loan for the furnishings, equipment, and start-up expenses. This way you can reduce your investment, and should the venture fail, reduce your loss. However, you may still be responsible for the term of your lease. If the building is leased for five years and your business fails in the first year, you will have to make the lease payments for the remaining four years or find a suitable tenant to sub-lease the space. You could also try to persuade the landlord to let you out of your lease.

The terms of the lease must be favorable for both the landlord and you. A short-term lease — five years, with an option to renew for additional five-year periods — is usually safest for a new operator. (For more information on leasing, see chapter 6, "Choosing Your Restaurant's Location." See also *Negotiate Your Commercial Lease,* another title in the Self-Counsel Business Series.)

### Renovation

Because building a new freestanding structure is rarely possible for a new restaurateur, we will concentrate on renovation of an existing structure, although many of the principles involved in renovation also apply to building from scratch. Once you have chosen your location (whether purchased or leased) you should have a building inspection done, and then decide on the changes you want to make to the premises to create your dream. Whether the changes are major and structural or only cosmetic, this is a good time to get a little advice from a designer. Many a stylish-looking restaurant is actually rather impractical in terms of floor plan and equipment. Consulting a designer at this point can save you the time, energy, and money you would have to

*The business plan: The financial plan* **39**

spend later on to "work around" design problems. For an in-depth discussion of restaurant design, see chapter 7, "Design and Renovation."

**Construction budget cost summary**

Your construction budget cost summary must be done in conjunction with your design plans for your location and with your building contractors. Managing a construction project can be a difficult matter of juggling various contractors, subcontractors, inspectors, and permit requirements. You must decide if you have enough knowledge to personally oversee the project, or if you'd prefer to use a general contractor whose responsibility is to bring the whole project together, on time and on budget. The choice depends on the scale of the work and on your own experience in the construction field. A general contractor might be a little more expensive, but hiring one is usually worth it. Also, when it comes to creating a capital budget, it is much easier to use costs taken from tenders for the complete project from several prospective general contractors than it is to piece it together yourself from a multitude of smaller cost estimates from all the various trades. Sample 1 details an average construction budget cost summary.

**KEY POINT**

A construction contract should include all costs (i.e., obtaining required permits, materials, labor, and installation of equipment), the time frames required to get the work done, and penalty clauses for lateness. To ensure that your contracts include all the relevant conditions, get a lawyer's advice. All work should be guaranteed not only to be completed to your liking, but also to meet the local building-code specifications, as well as to meet requirements for any permits or licenses your business may require (e.g., liquor, vending).

### 1.1b Equipment budget cost summary

Your menu, style of service, and the size, shape, and design of your restaurant will dictate your equipment needs. (See chapter 8, "Equipment and Furnishings," for more information on equipment.) Make up as complete a list as you can from your experience or with consulting

## *Sample 1*
## CONSTRUCTION BUDGET COST SUMMARY

**Back-of-House Construction or Renovation**

Electrical and lighting  _____
Plumbing  _____
Mechanical (including HVAC)  _____
Sprinklers  _____
Kitchen cooking equipment  _____
Kitchen refrigeration and freezers  _____
Drywall, finishes, ceramic in kitchen  _____
Labor  _____
Supervision  _____
Stainless steel fabricating (shelving and work stations)  _____

Subtotal  _____

**Front-of-House/Dinning Room Construction or Renovation**

Plumbing  _____
Furniture and fixtures  _____
Small wares  _____
Lighting  _____
Sound system  _____
Flooring  _____
Millwork  _____
Finishes (including painting, tiling, artwork)  _____
Specialty décor items  _____
Signage  _____
Bar system  _____
POS system  _____
Communication center (computer/fax/phones)  _____

Subtotal  _____

**TOTAL**  _____

help. If you are purchasing or leasing an existing restaurant, this list may be minimal. Rather than buying expensive equipment right at the beginning, you may want to work with what you already have, until the business is generating a positive cash flow. However, some equipment may actually be cost-effective to purchase if it can save you time and labor costs. Be sure to consider your fire-extinguishing and ventilation systems if you are upgrading an existing kitchen.

Be sure also to include office and storage needs, as well as the more obvious kitchen and front-of-house equipment. Take a look at Sample 2 for some ideas about the kinds of equipment you will need.

### 1.1c Furnishings, small wares, and opening inventory cost summaries

When compiling your start-up costs, you must budget for furniture, décor items, kitchen and bar small wares, and china, glassware, and cutlery inventories. It is recommended that you have one-and-a-half to two times the number of cutlery and silverware as seats. This is dependent on your menu and style of service. Food and beverage inventories must be decided on and costed out, usually with your chef's help. Don't forget you will need to use up a certain amount of your initial food inventory while training your staff. A minimum of one week's food inventory is a good rule of thumb when deciding how much to budget for use in staff training.

### 1.2 Soft costs

You also need to anticipate and budget for the intangible and sometimes hidden costs of opening a restaurant. Here is a brief list of the most common soft costs:

- Consulting fees
- Legal and accounting fees
- Permit fees
- Pre-opening labor costs
- Pre-opening insurance
- Pre-opening advertising
- Cash floats

# Sample 2
# EQUIPMENT LIST (Generic)

**For a medium to small restaurant**

| KITCHEN | BAR | FLOOR | SMALL WARES |
|---|---|---|---|
| • Exhaust fan with hood (approximately 4' x 10') <br> • Stove with ovens, griddle (optional) <br> • Salamander <br> • Charcoal broiler <br> • Deep fat fryer <br> • Convection oven <br> • Microwave oven (industrial strength) <br> • Steam table (Bain Marie) <br> • Salad table with "low boy" refrigeration <br> • Reach-in refrigerator <br> • Reach-in freezer <br> • Walk-in refrigerator (with compressors and shelving) <br> • Walk-in freezer (with compressors and shelving) <br> • Dry-storage shelving <br> • Stainless-steel worktables <br> • Prep sink (two compartments) plus hookup <br> • Hand sink plus hookup <br> • Dishwasher with dish racks and decking <br> • Ice machine | • Bar, with back-bar display <br> • Stools <br> • Beer refrigerators <br> • Service station with ice bin; water source and hand sink <br> • Pop system (post-mix or pre-mix) <br> • Draft system, keg room; refrigerated lines, taps <br> • Self-contained draft unit (single to triple keg sizes) <br> • Auto glass washer <br> • Glassware <br> • Glass storage shelves/racks <br> • Sound system <br> • TVs | • Point-of sale (POS) system <br> • Bus stations <br> • Coffee machine <br> • Espresso coffee machine <br> • Tables <br> • Chairs <br> • China <br> • Flatware <br> • Linen <br><br> **OFFICE** <br> • Desk <br> • Computer <br> • Filing cabinet (minimum 3 drawer, legal size) <br> • Safe (minimum 1-hour fireproof, document safe) <br> • Security system (installation cost plus monthly fee) | • Miscellaneous kitchen small wares (pots, pans, ladles, serving spoons, knives) <br> • Food processor (industrial strength) <br> • Meat slicer and/or grinder <br> • Storage bins (large flour type) <br> • Brute wagons <br> • Flat wagon <br> • Scales <br> • Equipment console <br> • Blender (industrial strength) <br> • Slushy machine <br> • First-aid kit <br> • Fire extinguishers |

43

### 1.2a Consulting fees

You may need to consult a number of professionals in the planning stages of your restaurant, including architects, engineers, interior and facility designers, and marketing planners. Approval of your building or renovation plans by an architect or engineer may be necessary to obtain building permits or other legal requirements in your local jurisdiction. Designers and marketing planners can be very useful — but also quite expensive. Sometimes these professionals work on a percentage fee of the overall construction budget and sometimes by the hour or day. Almost all professionals will meet with you to discuss a project before charging you for their time. Take this opportunity to be as clear as you can about the help you need, and don't be afraid to ask questions so that you can evaluate the fees being quoted to you.

### 1.2b Legal and accounting fees

You should get a lawyer's advice regarding a number of issues, including partnership agreements, lease negotiation, and incorporation. This type of professional advice is necessary. It would be foolish to go into a partnership without a legal partnership agreement or to sign a lease without letting your lawyer review it.

Accountants can help with your financial plan, setting up your accounting systems, tax advice, and year-end planning. Accountants must, in most jurisdictions, sign off on your business year-end for tax purposes.

Choose these professionals for their previous restaurant experience and be sure you understand their fee structures and exactly what you are paying for.

### 1.2c Pre-opening labor costs

Your hiring costs will include newspaper ads, application forms, interviewing time, training fees, and the cost of paying your staff while they are being trained — all of these can add up to more than expected. Budget carefully or you run the risk of a cash shortfall even before you open your doors.

### 1.2d Permit fees

These include building permits, vending permits, and liquor licenses, and all can be much more costly and complicated than you anticipate. Investigate first.

### 1.2e Pre-opening insurance

Be sure you have met with your insurance broker and planned not only for the insurance on your restaurant when it opens but also for your renovation and training period. Thieves don't wait until you're officially open to steal inventory. If a worker falls and injures himself or herself during renovation, will your insurance pay? Does your construction contract stipulate the general contractor must insure the job site? Your insurance broker must answer these questions. He or she should also be able to advise you on a prudent amount of coverage before you open your doors.

### 1.2f Pre-opening advertising, promotional, and printing costs

Are you planning to advertise your opening in the local newspaper? Print up menus and matches with your logo on them? Perhaps even put a "spot" on your local radio station? You must budget carefully for all these costs.

### 1.2g Cash floats

Don't forget the obvious (but frequently not budgeted for) cost of your cash floats. You may need as much as $500 to $700 on hand daily to be sure your bar or bars have enough change at the beginning of each shift to facilitate a smooth operation.

Your capital budget must comprise the total money required to open the restaurant, plus enough of a financial cushion so the business will not falter due to cash-flow difficulties in the first months. Next, you must show prospective investors where you plan to get this money and how you plan to repay it.

## 2. Investment Plan

In this portion of your business plan, you should detail all money required to start your restaurant, as well as the proposed sources of this money. It is unlikely that any investor will invest more in a project than the equity partners are planning to, and even then investors will expect any loan to be secured by other assets. How much of the money will you (and your partners) be providing directly and how much do you anticipate borrowing from investors? What is your strategy for paying back your investors, and how quickly do you anticipate being able to do so?

*The business plan: The financial plan* **45**

Banks and other financial institutions are reluctant to lend money to any "unknown" business venture, and restaurants have a relatively high failure rate. Generally, lenders want to know that they can recoup any losses due to bankruptcy or other disasters from the collateral they require to secure a loan — and that means lenders often require collateral of equivalent or greater value than the amount of the loan requested.

If you know a banker or investor from a prior successful business venture, by all means use this relationship to help finance your restaurant. Otherwise, be prepared to have to put up your house or some other valuable asset as collateral. You may have to sign personal guarantees that make you — not just your restaurant — responsible for the debt.

Shop around for the best deal you can get, and don't be afraid to try to renegotiate the terms of your loan or to have your name removed as a personal guarantor if the restaurant performs well in the first year or two.

## 3. Financial Statements

The next step is to create projected financial statements; specifically, a projected income statement, cash-flow analysis for at least the first year of operation, and pro forma balance sheet dated at the end of that first year. If you have limited accounting skills, enlist the aid of an accountant. The first financial statement to complete is the income statement.

### 3.1 The income statement

The income — or profit and loss (P & L) — statement is the most important financial document for the restaurant owner/operator or manager. This statement shows not only how your restaurant makes money (revenue), but also how you spend money (expenses) to generate revenue. Most important, it shows whether or not you made more than you spent. Sample 3 show the categories usually included on an income statement.

#### 3.1a Estimating your restaurant's revenue

The most difficult part of creating a projected income statement is estimating revenue. Start by establishing an "average check." How much, on average, will your customers spend in your restaurant? For an existing restaurant, the average check is calculated from "historical" data: that is, you'd divide the sales in a given period by the number of customers served in that period. Obviously, calculating the average check

**46**  *Start and run a restaurant business*

# *Sample 3*
# INCOME STATEMENT

| | Dollars $ | Percent % |
|---|---|---|
| **Sales** | | |
| Food | | |
| Beverage | | |
| Other | | |
| **Total Sales** | _____ | 100% |
| | | |
| **Cost of sales** | | |
| Food | | |
| Beverage | | |
| Other | | |
| **Total cost of sales** | _____ | _____ |
| **Gross Profit** | _____ | _____ |
| | | |
| **Controllable expenses** | | |
| Salaries and wages | | |
| Employee benefits | | |
| Direct operating expenses* | | |
| Music and entertainment | | |
| Marketing | | |
| Promotions | | |
| Heat, gas | | |
| Light, electric | | |
| Repair and maintenance | | |
| Administrative and general | | |
| Communications | | |
| **Total controllable expenses** | _____ | _____ |
| | | |
| **Fixed expenses** | | |
| Rent | | |
| Other occupation costs | | |
| Insurance | | |
| Licenses and memberships | | |
| **Total operating expenses** | _____ | _____ |
| | | |
| **Income before interest, depreciation, and taxes** | _____ | _____ |
| Interest | | |
| Depreciation | | |
| Net income before taxes | | |
| Income taxes | | |
| | | |
| **Net Income** | _____ | _____ |

*Direct operating expenses include the following categories, which can be separated out if an operator wants to track them individually: laundry and linens, china, glass and silverware replacement, paper supplies, bar supplies, menus, paper, postage, printing, legal services, office supplies, and landscaping.

for a restaurant that doesn't yet exist and for which, naturally, you have no sales data means you must use other methods.

First look at your proposed menu, but be aware that taking a simple average of your menu items' prices will not suffice. Many customers will have an appetizer with a meal but no dessert, or visa versa. However, there are two reliable ways you can determine an average check.

The first is to use focus groups, or surveys, of the people you have established are your target market. (See chapter 3, "The Business Plan: Feasibility Study," for information on target markets.) Simply ask them to choose what they would eat from your menu at a normal meal, then use this data to calculate your average check as if it were historical sales data.

The second method for calculating your average check is to take an average of your entire menu's entrées, disregarding both the most and least expensive items (like an ice-skating judge!), and do the same with your appetizers and desserts together. (In these health-conscious times, most people will have an appetizer or a dessert with dinner, but rarely both.) Add these two averages, and add the price of a coffee. You now can use this grand total as a crude, but fairly accurate, average check.

Calculate an average check for all your menus: breakfast, lunch, dinner, late night, and bar, as applicable. The average check for each meal will be different; people expect to spend different amounts, depending on the meal, and your prices should reflect this. When calculating the average check for lunch as well as late night and bar menus, do not include the appetizer and dessert average in the calculation. People do not eat as much at these times as they do at dinner.

If you sell alcoholic beverages, an average alcoholic beverage check must also be calculated for each meal period. Times are changing and alcoholic beverage sales at lunch are declining, so estimate one standard glass of house wine per every fourth customer at lunch. Estimate one standard glass of house wine per person at dinner. Some dinner customers will not drink, others will have two or three, but our experience in dining rooms is that the average check works out to approximately one glass of house wine each. Using a survey or focus group might give you a clearer picture, especially if you intend to have an expensive wine list. (If you anticipate selling alcoholic beverages as more than accompaniments to meals, see chapter 14, "Bars and Pubs.")

**48**   *Start and run a restaurant business*

When you have finished this exercise you should have an average check for food and an average check for alcoholic beverages for each of the meal periods you serve.

Now you must estimate the number of customers you expect to serve at each of these meal periods. This is called estimating your STR (seat turnover rate or ratio). In the restaurant business, you often hear STR described as covers, turns, or flips. Simply put, STR is the total customers served in a given meal period, divided by the number of seats you have in your restaurant. For example, if you have 100 customers at lunch and you have 100 seats, your STR at lunch was 1 ($100 \div 100 = 1$). If you have 50 customers at lunch, your STR would be 0.5 ($50 \div 100 = 0.5$).

Now, suppose you add up the STRs for all your lunches for a week and it comes to a total of 4.8. You need only multiply 4.8 by your 100 seats to know that you served 480 customers ($4.8 \times 100 = 480$) lunch during that week. By multiplying your 480 lunch customers by the average lunch food check, you can establish your lunch food revenue for that week. For example, let's use the amount $8.75 as your average lunch check. So 480 multiplied by $8.75 equals $4,200. Therefore, $4,200 would be your estimated lunch food revenue for that week.

If you add this figure to the totals for dinner-food revenue and the alcoholic beverage revenues for lunch and dinner, you now have a relatively accurate estimate of your total revenue for the week. Thus you can work up an estimate of your restaurant's annual revenue using your meal-period STRs and the meal-period average check amounts.

If you expect normal weekly, monthly, and seasonal fluctuations in your sales, you should predict your STR day by day or, at a minimum, week by week for the first year of business. Predicting how busy an as-of-yet-unopened restaurant is going to be must be done carefully and conservatively. You do not want to overestimate how busy the restaurant will be. Having relatively accurate estimates of your restaurant's revenue is the basis of a solid financial plan.

Projecting any STR — even for an existing restaurant with historical sales data from which to work — involves a certain amount of guessing. One way to help the accuracy of this guessing is to have a long hard look at how busy your closest competitors are. Go and observe the restaurants near your proposed restaurant's location. Pick the restaurants that are most similar to yours in concept and menu prices, the ones that attract the target market you are hoping to capture. Count

*The business plan: The financial plan* **49**

the customers they serve at lunch and dinner, on the slower weekdays and on the busiest, in high season and in low. Ask their wait staff how busy they get. A friendly bartender or waitress may give you valuable insight into the level of business you can expect at various times of day, days of the week, even seasonally in the area.

If you are familiar with the area, you might already have a good idea of the amount of business to expect. If not, do this research diligently. This is the heart of a critical decision point. If the business volume you anticipated does not seem to be evident, you must rethink the project. A possible exception is the introduction of a new concept (or, at least, new to the area) that might make your restaurant a destination in and of itself, and therefore not altogether dependent on the usual business volumes in the area. This type of restaurant actually creates its own niche through its colorful "personality" and uniqueness. Traditionally "bad" locations can become quite successful and, in turn, highly desirable in situations like this. Very trendy restaurants now exist in formerly decaying areas of cities; for instance, the meat-packing district on Manhattan's lower east side has become a trendy spot for restaurants. However, it usually takes a seasoned restaurant operator to pull off this type of move.

If, as you hoped, the business in the area looks strong, use the numbers you observe in your future competitors to help project STRs for your proposed restaurant. If your estimated revenue has a component that does not depend on the seating size of your restaurant — such as take-out food, off-premises catering, or stand-up bar business — then you must use means other then STR projections to predict it. Guestimating sales figures by square footage instead of number of seats is one option. However, your estimate of these types of sales should be conservative. Often it takes many months to establish your niche in the marketplace.

### 3.1b *Estimating your restaurant's expenses*

#### Cost of product

Once you have estimated your first year's revenue, you must estimate your expenses for that year.

Food costs and beverage costs can be estimated on a percentage basis. Find the cost percentages of your menu items by taking the cost of each item divided by the menu price of that item. (For more on cost

**50** *Start and run a restaurant business*

control, see chapter 13, "Cost Control.") The average of these percentages (again, throw out the highest and the lowest) can be used as a crude overall cost percentage. Do separate cost percentages for food and for alcoholic beverages.

These overall average cost percentages will be more accurate if you have done a survey or focus group on your menu. A focus group can be informal: just ask family and friends to participate, or extend an invitation to potential customers through local advertising or working with the business-improvement association in your area. Naturally, the more popular a menu item is, the more that item's cost percentage will influence the overall average. However, simply taking the overall average food cost percentage and multiplying it by your estimated food revenue and dividing by 100 will give you a general idea of your annual food cost. Alcoholic beverage costs can be estimated the same way.

### Labor cost calculations

Next, estimate your labor costs. A simple way to gage these costs is to make up a standard week's work schedule. Do not include salaried positions, as you already know the annual cost of these. After you have worked out how many hours are needed for the various positions required to run your restaurant for a week, multiply the hours for each position by the hourly rate you intend to pay for that position. Add the costs of all the positions together to get the "raw" dollar figure needed to staff your restaurant for a week.

Once you have costed out an average week's payroll, multiply the dollar amount by the number of weeks you will be open in the year, add in the annual salaries and an appropriate percentage for mandatory employee benefits, and you will have your rough annual labor cost. Government-required employee benefits — social security, employment insurance, and other mandatory payroll taxes — might be as much as 15 percent to 18 percent, so don't forget to add in these costs. Also add the cost of any benefits of your own choosing, such as employee meals.

If you anticipate fluctuations in seasonal business because of patio seating or tourist seasons or similar influences, naturally your labor requirements will change too. In such cases, it is appropriate to take a minimum of four interspersed weeks from throughout the year, and make up and cost schedules for each of these weeks. Then take the average of these as your average week's payroll. By using this average week's payroll in your calculations, you will have adjusted your labor cost predictions for these seasonal changes.

### Other operating expenses

Now you must list all the smaller expenses that you expect to incur over the course of the year. These expenses can vary widely depending on your location, the facilities you have available, the style of your restaurant, and many other factors. For example, if your restaurant is downtown in a large city, the cost of advertising and promotion might be quite different than they would be if you were in a small town or suburban community. Linen costs for a fine-dinning restaurant are substantially more than for a family diner.

If you are fortunate enough to have access to financial statements of other restaurants that are similar to your concept, these might give you some guidance in estimating some of these expenses.

### Fixed expenses

Fixed expenses are sometimes referred to as overhead. They do not fluctuate with sales volumes and can usually be estimated quite accurately. Some of them, such as rent, common-area expenses, property taxes, and insurance permit fees, can be taken directly out of your lease agreement. Others, such as depreciation, amortized pre-opening expenses, mortgage and/or note payable, and interest payable, can be estimated from your start-up costs and loan agreements.

### Income tax

Income tax is the final expense, and, of course, the amount you will have to pay depends on how much money you have made. Once you have estimated your restaurant's revenue, subtract all other expenses, and then apply the appropriate tax rate for your jurisdiction to the remainder to get an estimate of your tax owed.

## 3.1c  Profit

With the above information, you can now create a projected income statement for the first year. After you subtract all your expenses from your revenue, do you have a profit? Do you have enough profit to warrant continuing? You must decide.

## 3.2  The break-even analysis

The purpose of the break-even analysis is to calculate the minimum level of revenue your restaurant needs to generate in order to cover all its expenses. To perform this calculation, you must assign all your expenses into two categories: variable expenses and fixed expenses. Calculations of this type have certain limitations: for this calculation to remain valid, you must assume there will be minimal variation in any expenses you have categorized as "fixed" and that the economic climate will remain stable.

Fixed expenses are those expenses that do not vary with the volume of sales, such as rent or your mortgage payments. Variable expenses, as their name implies, are any expenses that alter or "vary" with the volume of sales. The prime example of a variable expense is cost of product: naturally, as your food sales increase, so too does your basic cost of food. You cannot sell a hamburger without incurring the cost of the hamburger meat, the bun, and condiments.

In an existing business, there are several complicated methods that can be employed using historical data to calculate what portion of the business's expenses are fixed and what portion are variable. For our purposes, however, we can use a much simpler technique to make the distinction.

Small- to medium-size restaurants tend to have relatively stable expense patterns. Food and beverage costs are, of course, variable, but virtually all other costs can be classified as fixed, with the exception of a small portion of the labor costs. As business increases, service staff and perhaps some kitchen staff are increased to cope with it. To calculate this variable amount of labor costs, we need only compare our projected payroll on the busiest week of the year to that of the slowest week of the year. The percentage difference between the two is the percentage of the labor cost that should be categorized as variable. Then, using the following formula, we can make a simple calculation to find how much we need to make in revenue:

$$\frac{\text{Fixed costs} \ + \ \text{Profit desired}}{100\% \ - \ \text{Variable costs (as a \% of revenue)}} \ = \ \text{Revenue}$$

Example:

Let's suppose that in our restaurant we have fixed costs of $150,000 annually, and the cost of food and beverages are 33% of total revenue. The cost of labor is 40% of total revenue. We estimate one-quarter of our labor cost is variable cost. One quarter of 40% = 10% of total revenue.

*The business plan: The financial plan* **53**

All variable costs then work out to be 43 percent (33% + 10%) of revenue, and we know fixed expenses equal $150,000. We will use zero as our profit figure since break-even is, by definition, the point at which we simply cover all our costs and have not yet made any profit. We apply the break-even formula to our example as follows:

$$\frac{\$150,000 \ + \ 0 \ \text{Profit}}{100\% \ - \ 43\% \ = \ 57\%} = \frac{\$150,000}{0.57} = \$ 263,157.89$$

We would need to make approximately $264,000 in sales annually just to cover all costs and break even.

## 3.3 The balance sheet

The next financial statement you must create for your financial plan is a pro forma balance sheet for the end of your first fiscal year. This will show potential investors the value of the assets of the restaurant and the predicted equity position. How much of the restaurant do you anticipate owning outright at the end of the first year, and how much will be "leveraged" by your liabilities? You must project the assets the restaurant will own after one year as well as the debts that will be incurred to acquire those assets. And, of course, you must project how much equity the owners will have compared to their debt at that time. Here again the advice of a professional accountant will be valuable. The same applies to the cash-flow analysis.

## 3.4 The cash-flow analysis

The cash-flow analysis shows the relationship between your current assets and your current liabilities. Current assets are assets that are "liquid" or will be liquidated — converted to cash — within 12 months (i.e., cash in the bank, cash floats, accounts receivable, and inventories). Current liabilities, similarly, are debts that must be paid within 12 months (i.e., accounts payable, the current portion of your mortgage, and interest). Your cash-flow analysis indicates your ability to meet your short-term debts. Naturally, the larger your current assets are compared to your current liabilities, the better you appear to a prospective lender.

A cash-flow analysis is sometimes not included in the financial plans for restaurants. Restaurants, unlike most retail or manufacturing businesses, often have few accounts receivable, since most suppliers will usually give modest terms and allow some time to pay their bills and since most restaurant customers pay for their meals immediately in cash. (Major credit-card receivables are usually considered as good as cash). Restaurants usually are in the enviable business position of "working on their suppliers' capital," and thus have a naturally positive cash flow.

There are situations, however, in which this may not be the case. Private clubs, for instance, may have cash-flow difficulties because they are not able to collect their receivables quickly enough to cover their short-term debts. New restaurants with no credit history may have difficulty getting terms from their suppliers and might suffer cash-flow problems. This is the primary reason we consider it still worthwhile to include a cash-flow analysis in your financial plan. It helps put a prospective lender's mind a little more at ease.

Cash-flow shortages in new restaurants are common but they tend to be due to undercapitalization. Often the capital needed to open the restaurant is underestimated and/or the initial projected sales volume is too optimistic. This is why you must take great pains to ensure that the capital budget for opening your restaurant is as accurate as possible. The same applies to your financial projections. Better to be conservative and underestimate sales objectives than to be overconfident and run into cash-flow problems. It is not uncommon for new restaurants not to make any profit in the first year of operation!

The information and statements summarized above will form the basis for your financial plan. This, along with your feasibility study and marketing plan, completes your business plan. Now you have the tools to meet the challenge of financing a new restaurant project.

Completing your business plan can sometimes be a struggle. Don't become discouraged! Lenders and agents of financial institutions are a conservative lot. Independent restaurant projects have a well-deserved reputation as bad risks. Have faith in your dream and in the preparation work you have done. Institutional lenders are not the only source of money. Private lenders, new "silent" partners, or limited partnerships are all possible alternative sources of capital.

# 4. Resources

Following is a list of resources that may be of use to you in drawing up your business plan and finding funding.

### US Small Business Administration (SBA)

The US Small Business Administration provides financial, technical, and management help to enable Americans to start and run their own businesses. It offers a number of programs and services, including training and educational programs, counseling services, and financial and contract assistance. Companies such as Ben and Jerry's Ice Cream and Nike got their start with the help of the SBA. Consult the US Government section of your telephone directory to find the office nearest you, or visit <www.sba.gov> on the Web.

### Canadian Bankers Association (CBA)

The CBA provides information to the public on industry and financial issues through its program Building a Better Understanding. Publications are available on money management, interest rates, and starting a small business. To obtain copies, call toll free 1-800-263-0231 or visit <www.cba.ca> on the Web. You can also order by writing to Building a Better Understanding, c/o Canadian Bankers Association, Box 348, Commerce Court West, 199 Bay St., 30th floor, Toronto, Ontario M5L 1G2.

The following are addresses of Canadian bank Web sites that have information for small-business people:

| | |
|---|---|
| Bank of Montreal | www.bmo.com |
| Bank of Nova Scotia | www.scotiabank.ca |
| Canadian Imperial Bank of Commerce | www.cibc.com |
| Royal Bank of Canada | www.royalbank.com |
| Toronto Dominion Bank | www.tdbank.ca |

### Small Business Consumer Centre

The Small Business Consumer Centre is the largest research centre of its kind in Canada and tracks government programs available to Canadian entrepreneurs. Contact them for a copy of their kit entitled *Getting Government Money*, which includes a video (*How to Apply for Grants and*

*Loans*), the *Grants, Loans and Assistance* guide, a package of sample applications, *A Business Plan Success Strategies Workbook,* and *The Grantsmanship Report.* You can call the Small Business Consumer Centre by phone at 1-800-667-1493; write to them at 458 Richmond Street West, Toronto, ON M5V 1Y1; or visit them on the Web at <www.grants-loans.com/>.

### Western Economic Diversification Canada

Western Economic Diversification Canada concentrates its efforts on developing the economy of Western Canada, but provides a number of on-line, interactive information products to small-business people and entrepreneurs. You can find them on the Web at <www.wd.gc.ca>.

### Canada Revenue Agency Information for Small Business

Canada Revenue Agency produces *The Guide for Canadian Small Business,* a user-friendly guide to assist entrepreneurs in setting up small businesses and understanding Canada Revenue Agency's programs and initiatives. Visit them on the Web at <www.cra-arc.gc.ca>.

### Business Nation

This is a Web site for businesses and entrepreneurs. It contains much useful information for the businessperson, plus links to other resources on the Web <www.businessnation.com>.

### Business Lenders

Business Lenders are "committed to providing small businesses with the funds they need to achieve success." It is affiliated with the SBA and can lend from $100,000 to $5,000,000. Find them on the Web at <www.businesslenders.com>.

# Part 2
# START-UP

The start-up period can hold some of the most thrilling experiences in your life as a restaurant operator. You have already invested a great deal of time and energy in a project that has, up to this point, been just a dream. Suddenly finances come together, and the feasibility study, market analysis, and pro forma financial statements are all completed. Now it is time for you to select a site that fits your concept and decide whether to buy or lease the premises. You agonize over the choice of the restaurant's name; you obtain the necessary licenses and permits. You begin sourcing equipment, and you are shocked at the quickly mounting costs and are forced either to return to the sources of capital funds to seek further assistance or to look for alternatives to your original plans. You begin to hire your senior employees, and you work through your plans with them in anticipation of your opening-night audience.

The next five chapters will take you through the start-up process, beginning with issues such as naming your restaurant and selecting a site that will best support your concept. To increase your chances for success, your restaurant's site, theme, design, and overall style of operation must all be compatible. The last chapter in this section will deal with your employees and the human resources challenges that await you.

Welcome to Start-Up.

# Chapter 5
# START-UP PRACTICALITIES

The practicalities of the start-up period include choosing a name for your restaurant; registering your business; and obtaining licenses, permits, and insurance. This work takes patience, but it is necessary to ensure the successful opening of your business.

## 1. Naming Your Restaurant

The name of your restaurant is part of its image and should match its concept, theme, and service style. Your name can help tell your story and may let customers know what to expect. In deciding on a name for your restaurant, there are three primary considerations: Your own tastes, marketing implications, and copyright.

### 1.1 *Your own tastes*

You should pick a name that you like and with which you have some affinity. After all, this is your dream, not someone else's. Remember: with luck, you'll be living with the name for a long time.

### 1.2 Marketing implications

The marketing implications of the name you choose are a major consideration. You want the name of your restaurant to be striking and memorable, and to evoke in some way the concept your restaurant embodies. Catchy or funny names can benefit family-style restaurants and bars and pubs, but be careful of using them if you want to make a serious statement with your fine-dining cuisine. It may imply to some that you're not really serious about your food. A foreign family name or even a foreign word or phrase is often used to imply a type of cuisine: for instance, "Roma" or "Amarone" with Italian food, or "Zapata's" for Mexican food. A name that has local or regional historical significance is another method of connecting a restaurant to its community. There are firms that specialize in "naming," and if you have exhausted all your possibilities and still have come up without a name that works, it may be wise to use the talents of a local marketing company that specializes in name development.

In the 1980s, co-author Brian Floody was the co-owner and operator of a local restaurant in Toronto situated on land that had been the site of the first dial-telephone exchange in Canada. The restaurant was called The Grover Exchange, after the name of the original telephone exchange. A telephone-dial logo and a collection of antique telephones were used in the decor to reflect the telephone theme.

### 1.3 Copyright

Be sure that you make a copyright name search of the name that you hope to use for your restaurant, especially if you think you might expand beyond one location or even franchise your concept if the first location is a success. A lawyer specializing in copyright law can provide you with this service, or a visit to city hall can also confirm whether your proposed name has already been registered by another business. To start, you may want to consult the business Yellow Pages in your area and review the names of restaurants already operating in your municipality to avoid duplication and disappointment.

## 2. Registering Your Business

### 2.1 In the United States

In all states, any person who uses a name other than a surname to identify a business must register the name with the state or county as an assumed or fictitious name. If you fail to register, you'll have all sorts of problems. For example, you may be unable to open a bank account in your business name. You also may be barred from signing a contract with the name.

To register your business, you must file a certificate with the county clerk stating who is doing business under the name. In many states, you must publish the statement in a local newspaper. This is intended to help creditors identify the person behind an assumed business name, and makes it easier to track down those people who are in the habit of changing their business names to confuse and avoid creditors. You can also get information about the requirements for registering a business in your state from your particular state's Department of Revenue. The Web site <www.aicpa.org/yellow/yptsgus.htm> will link you to your state's Department of Revenue.

Some communities have newspapers that specialize in publishing such legal notices; your county clerk should be able to give you this information. Some states require that instead of, or in addition to, publication, you file the statement with the state Department of Revenue or some other state agency.

Contact your county clerk and ask about the registration requirements in your area. You'll have to fill out a simple form and pay a fee — usually no more than $15 to $50. The county clerk will normally check to see if any identical or very similar names have already been registered in the county. If so, you'll have to use another name. It's a good idea to think of several possible names before you attempt to register.

**KEY POINT:** If the name you have chosen is available, see if the state will let you reserve it. Most states will allow you to reserve a corporate name for a period of time, provided that the name isn't already in use or already reserved.

## 2.2 In Canada

In Canada, you should file and protect the name you have chosen. You can always operate your restaurant under your proper name (e.g., Joe Green's Café), but if you choose a fictitious name (e.g., Café Paris), most jurisdictions require that the name be registered. This is done by filing a "fictitious name statement" with the provincial authorities. When you register a fictitious name, it will be checked against previously filed names to ensure that the name has not been taken by another business. This is for your protection, too. Once your name is on file, it cannot be used by anyone else.

You can have a name search done through the provincial ministry that handles incorporations. This will also tell you if the name is registered out of province. This process takes about a week, and there is a small fee, generally under $50.

# 3. Trademarks

If you plan to use a trademark (a logo, graphic, set of initials, or word) in connection with your restaurant, you would be well advised to register it, in order to prevent another company using the same or a similar mark. For more information on trademarks, in the United States contact the Patent and Trademark Office (PTO) at 800-786-9199 or 703-308-4357, or on the Web at <www.uspto.gov>. In Canada, contact the Canadian Intellectual Property Office at 819-997-1936 or via the Web at <www.strategis.ic.gc.ca/sc_mrksv/cipo/>.

# 4. Obtaining Licenses and Permits

It is essential to obtain all the necessary licenses and permits so that you do not have any delays in opening your restaurant. Investigate the procedure for applying for all permits and licenses through your city- or town-hall economic development office or county clerk's office. Permits for liquor will vary by city and state or province, so you will need to investigate and identify those that are necessary in your location. A lawyer and an accountant can assist you in complying with all state, federal, and local laws. Be certain to get your liquor licenses before opening your restaurant. Remember, also, that your contractors will need to secure the proper permits for any construction work you have planned.

# 5. Insurance

Your restaurant is your livelihood and is a major investment. It must be protected, and therefore you must have the proper insurance. If you are leasing a property, your landlord will be responsible for insuring the building (though he or she will pass those charges on to you in your rent). However, you are responsible for obtaining insurance on the contents and for obtaining your own liability insurance. You should also consider insurance to cover business interruption as well as key personnel surety and fidelity bonding. Discuss with your broker the different kinds of insurance you are likely to need.

Here are some tips on obtaining insurance:

☞ Consider using an independent insurance broker. An independent broker works for you to fulfill the risk-management needs of your establishment. Unlike an agent working directly for an insurance company, independent brokers are not necessarily trying to sell you the insurance package most advantageous to the insurance company. Approach finding a good insurance broker as you would search for any other supplier. Use word of mouth, ask your restaurant association for recommendations, and always ask for references.

☞ Your local restaurant association may have information about insurance packages specifically tailored for restaurants. Some insurance companies that specialize in restaurant coverage may be able to offer excellent packages to suit your specific needs.

☞ Do *not* try to insure yourself against every minor accident. An insurance broker once told co-author Brian Floody that money spent on insurance was "worth about 60 cents on the dollar." So insure your restaurant against major catastrophes, fire, flood, major disasters, but "don't sweat the small stuff." Numerous minor claims for vandalism or breakage will only push up your premiums and could even make it difficult for you to renew your insurance. Instead of trying to cover everything, take a large deductible, a minimum of $1,000, which will help keep your premiums down, and increase your repairs-and-maintenance budget to cope with any minor damages or thefts. In the long run, you will save money.

*Start-up practicalities* **67**

☞ Do carry at least two million dollars in liability insurance, especially if you are planning to serve alcohol. Third-party-liability damage awards have been climbing all over North America, and you don't want to be underinsured in this area.

☞ Be certain you are not double insured. Your broker can talk to your landlord to find out what his or her building insurance covers and then design an insurance package for you that will not insure something already covered by your landlord's policy. (You are often paying indirectly for such coverage in rent or "common area" payments anyway.)

☞ If you have antiques or furnishings that may be difficult to assess or may appreciate in value over time, keep a photographic record of them. Even a home-video tape with a voiceover describing the pieces and what you paid for them will be invaluable in case of disaster. Give a copy of the tape to your insurance broker and keep a copy of the tape at home!

# Chapter 6
# CHOOSING YOUR RESTAURANT'S LOCATION

Location! Location! Location! These are the three most important factors in determining the success of your restaurant, so take your time when choosing where to establish your operation. This is a critical decision point; the wrong location can be disastrous, just as the right location can launch your success.

## 1. Finding the Fit

Your choice of a site will depend heavily on your concept and style of restaurant. The key is having the right "fit" — location and restaurant type must be complimentary, and you will need patience as you search for that perfect fit. Your understanding of the marketplace and its demographics is crucial to your site-selection process, and the information gathered in your feasibility study (see chapter 3, "The Business Plan: Feasibility Study") will help to clarify whether or not a particular site is right for your restaurant. Here are some important factors to consider when choosing your site and assessing the fit:

- *Area demographics.* Do they meet your customer profile? (Refer to your feasibility study.) Will the population base support your restaurant? Is the site near offices? Are there sporting venues, theaters, residential neighborhoods, and other demand generators nearby? The activity from these businesses will contribute to your customer base and increase your sales.

- *Visibility.* You will need optimum visibility from the street or highway for signage to attract maximum pedestrian and car traffic. It is best if the restaurant can at least be viewed from both sides of the street.

- *Positioning on the street in relation to other complimentary businesses.* Are you on the fringe of the "prime" location or in the heart of that district? In some locations, being on the "right" side of the street may have considerable impact. Accessibility from a highway or street is critical to attracting maximum potential customers.

- *Accessibility.* Ease of parking or proximity to public parking lots is paramount if you are in a city or downtown location. You will need adequate parking to meet any local building codes. Parking can be a very sensitive issue for customers; their decision on where to dine is often influenced by the ease of parking. Some restaurants offer valet parking, especially if they are in a city location with no parking lot or minimal street parking.

- *Desirability of surroundings.* Or can your operation be the catalyst that will transform a traditionally undesirable location into a new "in" spot? This takes courage and usually would need a seasoned operator with a history and a loyal clientele willing to follow him or her to the new location.

- *Convenience.* Proximity to work or residences of your potential clientele will help you establish yourself as "the" neighborhood spot. You can work to cultivate the business sector at lunchtime by setting up house charge accounts, taking orders by fax, and perhaps establishing yourself as their off-site meeting place.

- *Competition from comparable restaurants.* Is there still room in the existing marketplace for another restaurant (yours)? Has there been demonstrated growth and economic stability in the area? Often, the more restaurants there are in an area, the better their chances of creating a "restaurant row" situation. Having a number of restaurants together may add to the total market because people will come a greater distance to a restaurant row than to separately located restaurants. A word of caution, though: a restaurant row requires a large population base.

The greater the area's demand, the higher the price that will be charged for that location, but you should review this cost–value relationship. Perhaps being just outside the prime real estate location will allow you to operate at significantly lower overhead and yet still be within the catchment area.

## 2. Downtown versus Suburban

The choice of a downtown or city location versus a suburban one may confront you. There are advantages to both locations. Keep the following considerations and advantages and disadvantages of each in mind as you make your decision:

### 2.1 Suburban

One of the advantages of a suburban location is that parking is not an issue. As well, land is less expensive, and therefore the cost of purchasing or leasing will be less per square foot. The cost of labor may be lower, you may have an easier commute, and you will be able to have more space for seating, bars, storage, and possibly banquets, all of which can increase your revenue. You can become involved with the local community and support town events (children's softball, soccer, etc.).

There are some disadvantages to a suburban setting. You will be relying on the local population for support, so your understanding of the demographics and competition will be crucial to your success. There will be very few, if any, walk-in customers. Driving is the mode of transportation in the suburbs, so drinking and your liquor-law liability will be a greater issue. You will have little diversity in your clientele and will be relying mostly on repeat business. Business volume could be uneven: it may be very slow during the week, but your restaurant could be packed on the weekends. Staff must have a car or ride to get to and from work.

*Choosing your restaurant's location* **71**

## 2.2 Downtown/City

Advantages of being located downtown are that you'll have a large customer base from which to draw, and there will be lots of walking traffic. City dwellers eat more weekday meals out than their suburban counterparts. Staff can take public transportation, so a car isn't essential for them to get to work. Many city dwellers entertain in restaurants, since they live in apartments that usually have small kitchens. City dwellers also are often a more sophisticated clientele who are willing to experiment with foods; therefore, your chef may have more room for creativity.

There are, however, disadvantages to city locations, which have a higher cost per square foot, smaller space, and limited storage facilities. The cost of doing business will also be higher than in a suburban setting. (However, you may also charge higher prices than your suburban counterparts.) There will be limited parking, if any.

# 3. Freestanding versus Mall Location

Again, you must decide on the best location for your style and concept of restaurant. If you choose a mall, make certain the other tenants share a similar character and style and attract a type of clientele that matches your target market. However, if you decide to be part of a food court within a shopping mall, carefully consider the other food tenants and decide how you will distinguish yourself from them.

Operating outside the traditional site-selection rules — location and convenience — can be risky but rewarding if your restaurant has the right combination of value, service, food quality, décor, and sense of entertainment. Generally, it's the high-end, chef-driven, table-service restaurants that need not place such a high priority on location or convenience. Rather, they frequently create their own location and are successful in spite of traditionally "poor" — in the conventional sense of the word — sites. The owner's courage and risk taking is rewarded in terms of savings from the lower per-square-foot lease price or lower purchase price. These are the restaurants that often become the catalyst for transforming neighborhoods or areas that initially weren't considered ideal for restaurants or businesses into highly desirable locations.

"Destination" restaurants will be sought out because of some very special or unique combination of qualities — food, service, decor, or staff. Once your reputation has been established, your guests will drive, fly, train, boat, or use just about any other mode of transportation to get to you. In this case, the location is secondary. The business is not driven or reliant on a "prime" location, but rather stakes its claim as an exceptional dining experience. A guest must feel it's worth going that extra mile to reach your establishment and then want to spread the word and promote this find.

## 4. Zoning

You must be aware of current zoning regulations and restrictions that might affect your operation (e.g., hours, liquor, and the adjacent zoning laws). A visit to the municipal planning department or city hall is a good way to start, and is a step that you can eliminate only at your peril!

The following story from co-author Brian Cooper illustrates how a restaurant received a devastating blow when the owners discovered it was in a "dry" area and no liquor licenses could be issued to businesses in that location. It proves that you can't overestimate the importance of checking zoning regulations before making a major investment:

*While designing a series of unique rail restaurants for Canadian Pacific Hotels using some of the most unique stations situated in the middle of some of Canada's most beautiful cities, we found an ideal and design-perfect facility in western Toronto. It was truly a gem, and would have become the leading example of a railway restaurant. The architects and designers added four vintage rail cars to the design. The financial feasibility was perfect. After making a major investment in drawings and promotion, we applied for a building permit, only to discover that the building was situated in a small area zoned "liquor licenses prohibited." The investment of $250,000 was wasted, and now only the drawings remain.*

## 5. Leasing versus Purchasing

To minimize investment and risk, it is often wise to lease or buy an existing restaurant as opposed to starting from ground zero and building a new one. It is a less daunting task to take over and renovate an existing restaurant already equipped with the basics. Purchasing may be an option only if your restaurant is in an outlying area where the cost of real estate is still affordable, rather than in a major urban center. Owning does offer the opportunity to make a sizeable return on your investment when you decide to sell the business, especially if the restaurant has been successful. There are situations in which a building might be appreciating quickly due to local market conditions and the purchase of the building might be a solid business opportunity over and above the viability of your restaurant project. However, these situations are rare, and financing them can be difficult, so we will concentrate here on leasing the appropriate space. Leasing involves, naturally, substantially less capital investment than purchasing.

The cost of a lease in a mall or business/shopping concourse may be based on gross sales, with a fixed minimum amount per square foot per month. In this case, the lease payments will increase or decrease in proportion to the gross revenue generated each month. This scenario may be acceptable and appealing in the early phases of growing your business; however, should your restaurant take off, it's the landlord who will capture the windfall! In such a situation, rent/lease payments will be considered a "variable" expense (see chapter 4, "The Business Plan: The Financial Plan"). You may find a fixed-rate lease agreement with a ten-year term and an option to renew to be the most desirable arrangement, but your location and local real estate practices may dictate the terms of your lease. Rosemary Lee, a friend of co-author Gina McNeill, owns several restaurants in Hong Kong and says it is difficult to obtain a lease there for more than one year! Rosemary has found success by situating her operations on the edge of prime areas, thereby receiving substantial reductions in leasing costs, but still benefiting from proximity to the most desirable locations.

Sometimes you can simply negotiate a new lease with the landlord if the premises are currently vacant, or you can purchase an existing lease from a tenant. Either scenario calls for legal advice. Leases are complex documents, and making a mistake when signing one can drastically impede your success before you even get started! Here are a few examples of things to consider before signing a lease:

(a) *How long should the lease run?* The longer the term of your lease, the better. If the rent is reasonable and your restaurant is successful you don't want to be forced out by the end of a lease. This is a more common scenario than you might think.

**74**  *Start and run a restaurant business*

Years ago an acquaintance of co-author Brian Floody's who had worked as a cook for some time decided to invest his savings in a small specialty fish-and-chip shop in a busy area of town. He bought the last two years of a five-year lease on an existing restaurant that had closed its doors. He found himself in a very favorable market, and over the first 18 months built up a thriving business. He then approached his landlord for what he assumed would be an automatic extension of the lease, at perhaps a slightly higher rent. He was shocked to discover the landlord had no plans to extend his lease and indeed intended to take over the location at the end of the remaining six months and let his son run a fish-and-chip shop in what appeared to be a great location for one!

If your business does not succeed as you anticipate, having a long lease gives you an asset that you can sell, and it might turn out to be more valuable than your business goodwill and your equipment and chattels! Which brings us to the next important element of a lease.

(b) *Can you transfer ownership of the lease if you decide to sell your business?* This depends completely on the lease agreement. Be sure that your lease agreement allows this. If the landlord insists he or she must give his or her permission to transfer the lease, add a clause that states, "Permission not to be unreasonably withheld." If you cannot transfer the lease to a future purchaser of your business, even if the lease allows the sale of your restaurant, you will continue to be liable for any default on the part of the new business owner on the terms of the lease.

(c) *Can you cancel the lease if for some reason you cannot open your restaurant?* The answer is a resounding NO, unless you avail yourself of protective "escape clauses." The term escape clause refers to a variety of clauses commonly added to lease agreements (or any other type of contract) that allow one party or the other to be released if certain conditions or requirements are not met or do not come to pass. Naturally, you and your lawyer will attempt to negotiate as few escape clauses or required conditions as possible for the landlord, and the landlord in turn will resist clauses that might allow you to escape from a signed lease. But certain conditions are essential for you to be able to carry on a normal business, and you dare not sign a lease agreement unless you can ensure that these conditions are in place.

A commonly used escape clause in any real estate contract is an "ability to obtain financing" provision. This is often used in commercial restaurant leasing. Usually a lender will not commit to backing a project that has not secured a location. Most lenders will require a signed lease agreement to show that a proposed restaurant has "locked in" its location and is able to proceed. Naturally, the ability to proceed with the project depends on the ability to obtain financing from the lender. In order to avoid falling into this "catch 22," most landlords will allow a certain period of time after signing a lease agreement in which to secure financing. If the financing cannot be secured for some other reason, the lease becomes null and void.

One of the most commonly overlooked conditions is the importance of being able to gain a liquor license. At least half a dozen times during co-author Brian Floody's consulting career, he has been contacted by people who have signed a long lease on a property, only to find out that they could not get a liquor license. Too late they realized they were now responsible for a number of years of rent, whether they could open their restaurant or not.

Many restaurant concepts depend on the ability to sell beverage alcohol and cannot be competitive without it. Liquor laws can be complex and arbitrary. They differ from state to state and province to province. Make certain that your lease agreement allows you to be released from the contract if it becomes impossible for you to obtain a liquor license or, for that matter, meet any other legal requirement to do business. Zoning laws, building codes, and fire and health regulations will all have an impact on your business. Don't take any of them for granted when signing a lease agreement. As mentioned earlier, now is an excellent time to get good legal advice from a lawyer with restaurant real estate experience.

# Chapter 7
# DESIGN AND RENOVATION

## 1. Building Your Dream

Once you have decided on a location for your restaurant, you must either build it if it is to be a new stand-alone structure, or renovate it if you are converting an existing space into a new restaurant. Either way, the first step is design.

Careful design is crucial to creating the ambiance — the look and feel you want — and yet still ensuring that your space can offer you maximum efficiency in the production and service of your menu items. The placement and design of the kitchen is a critical part of your planning process. The balance between the complexity and style of the menu, seating capacity, and the size and configuration of the kitchen is essential. Your kitchen should be designed to meet the needs of its busiest period.

If you are building a new structure, building codes will most likely require the use of an architect. Even if you are only renovating an existing space, your local building codes will often require some architectural consulting if walls, plumbing, or exits are being altered. Be cautious about this, though. Architects understand the building-code requirements of your space, but they may know very little about how a restaurant functions. The use of an experienced restaurant facilities designer might be of great value.

## 2. *What Designers Can Do For You*

How big should your kitchen be? How much storage space should you have? How much cold storage and freezer space do you need? Exactly what kind of equipment will you need? Where should the equipment be placed? How much electricity, gas, water, and ventilation does each piece of equipment require? The answers to these and a thousand other questions will depend on the type of menu you have, the type of service you are planning, the size of your restaurant, and many other variables. An experienced facilities designer can help you answer them.

Often we have heard restaurateurs say, "I know the 'feeling' I want my guests to have, but I don't know how to get that feeling into the room." Experienced interior designers know how to create this "feeling."

In most good restaurants, ambiance is no accident. Much time and effort goes into selecting the right colors and décor, as well as the furnishings, china, linen, and flatware to complement them. Lighting is a vital design element, since its proper placement will highlight all your design efforts. But this ambiance must come from *your* ideas — your "concept." The more detailed a concept you can develop, the easier it will be for you to describe to a designer exactly what you want. You must be happy with the final result. You are the one who is going to have to live with it! So don't let designers or anyone else take you too far away from the way you've envisioned your restaurant.

## 3. **Design**

We have seen far too many restaurants that look wonderful but never seem to be able to provide good food and service. This often has to do with the fact that the physical design of the restaurant puts obstacles in the way of fast, efficient service: kitchens too far away from seating areas; bus stations or cash registers that make the service staff walk miles to place orders and then walk miles in another direction to pick them up; bars with too little storage space and with no way to restock them during busy periods except by pushing through the customers, to name just a few. A little good advice at this point can save you time, energy, and the money you would have to spend later on to work around design problems.

Both interior and facilities designers can help you realize your concept, not only in terms of ambiance but also in terms of functionality.

*Interior designers* are the better known of these two types. As mentioned above, their primary function is to create a "feel" for the space your restaurant occupies. The use of colors, shapes, and textures, and the effective use of space to create the ambiance your concept needs are their real strengths. The American Society of Interior Designers (ASID) is their 30,000-member–strong trade association and might be a valuable resource if you are in the market for one. You can find them on the Web at <www.asid.org/> or call them at 202-546-3480. In Canada, try the Interior Designers of Canada (IDC), on the Web at <www.interiordesigncanada.org> or by phone at 416-594-9310. You can also contact the International Interior Designers Association, on the Web at <www.iida.org> or by phone at 312-467-0779 or 888-799-4432.

*Facilities designers,* however, are specialists in functional layouts of serving areas, preparation areas, and kitchens. They can be an invaluable source of information about your equipment needs, water and power requirements, storage requirements, and other more functional details. If you need this kind of help, your local restaurant equipment supplier or restaurant association are good starting points. The Foodservice Consultants Society International (on the Web at <www.fcsi.org> or by phone at 502-583-3783) is another valuable resource. Cini-Little (on the Web at <www.cinilittle.com> or by phone at 301-528-9700) is also a well-respected international consulting firm specializing in foodservice equipment, layout, and design.

The trend in restaurant design today has been toward the open-concept or display kitchen. The display kitchen provides a degree of entertainment for customers and gives guests a perception of freshness, or an especially-made-for-me feeling, thus adding value to the dining experience. Prep kitchens for washing and chopping vegetables and cleaning meats and fish are often located behind the display kitchen, out of the customer's line of vision, but prep kitchens need to be close by so that they can "feed" the display-cooking station.

*Design and renovation* **79**

Because of this trend, the kitchen equipment has now become part of the overall look and design of the restaurant. Dessert islands or stations, seafood bars, rotisserie grills, and pasta-making machines have all become part of the American restaurant scene. Customers are using all their senses: smelling, seeing, tasting, and feeling their dining experience. Many restaurants today also include a retail or take-out space to generate additional revenue and capture some of the emerging home-meal replacement market.

**KEY POINT:** How do you choose a designer? The answer is, with care! Think about your restaurant concept. Who is your target market? Develop your ideas about your proposed restaurant in as much detail as possible. Know, as best you can, what you need before you begin to interview any kind of consultant. Many people offer professional advice for money, and many of them leave much to be desired. When you are looking for a designer, use a reliable source. Often word of mouth can be your best resource. Find restaurants that you like and ask who designed them. Have your friends or colleagues used someone with whom they were happy? Your local restaurant association might be able to recommend designers. A provincial or state association of interior designers might recommend someone specializing in restaurants.

But even with a good recommendation, you should ask any designer you are considering to provide a CV, and then you should check references to see whether or not your prospective designer has experience with restaurants — specifically, with restaurants similar in concept and style to the type you plan to open.

A good designer will be able to "read your mind" (so to speak), understand your concept, and help you realize that vision. The design and image of the restaurant must match your clientele's level of sophistication so that they are able to achieve a true comfort level within the restaurant space.

Designers may charge a flat fee per project or charge a percentage of the project's total cost. Food service is a specialized area, and your design team should include people with expertise in this field. Visit sites that the designers have worked on and speak with the owners about their experience with the designers.

# 4. Decor

The combination of materials, colors, textures, shapes, and lighting in your restaurant must all work together to project your style and be consistent with your concept. If they are not, you may be sending a confusing message to your customers, and they will not feel comfortable, nor will they return. Budgetary problems often arise during the construction or renovation stage, and changes need to be made to reduce costs — sometimes seriously compromising the original message or design feeling. But overspending on materials and finishes can stretch the budget too far and drive costs up so much that the financial health of the business becomes too severely compromised to recover. Checks and balances must be in place here, and ego must be left at the door.

Because kitchens are now sometimes integrated into the main part of the dining room and the equipment is becoming part of the decor, functionality and design have become important in today's equipment selection. Manufacturers have responded to this trend and are producing very stylized pieces of equipment. The French company, Bonnet, has developed a cutting-edge line of upscale display-cooking equipment, from rotisseries to customized full islands, complete with induction, flattops, open grills, and salamanders that can be accessed by chefs from both sides. The Culinary Institute of America at Graystone in Nappa Valley, California, has been outfitted with this complete line. This design idea has moved into the home kitchen as well. Commercial cooking equipment has become part of the upscale designer-home kitchen.

# 5. Designing without a Designer

If it is not feasible for you to hire a designer, put the word out to your friends and family. You can always ask your greatest supporters if they have any contacts in the field — in short, do they know someone with design expertise who may be willing to help you pull your ideas together? In addition, here are a few low-budget suggestions for decorating your restaurant:

☞ Use greenery and plants to improve the look of your space. However, be certain you can maintain and take care of them. Nothing looks worse than plants that are dusty and in serious need of watering.

*Design and renovation* **81**

☞ Display the work of local artists on your walls, in exchange for the visibility you can offer them.

☞ Scour the thrift shops for "props" that you can incorporate into your decor. Old kitchen small wares and interesting platters can sometimes be found at garage sales or antique markets.

☞ Check with your liquor sales rep about getting interesting bottles for display.

☞ Create ambiance by displaying memorabilia that fits your theme.

Table arrangements will depend on your clientele. Are you attracting families? Young professional couples? Baseball or soccer teams? Singles? Some restaurants that are located in urban city centers where traveling singles dine have been successful in setting up a large table at which individuals can join other single diners. Often these tables are located near an open kitchen, similar to a sushi-bar concept, so that there is some activity to watch. Using tables that can be easily moved also enables you to accommodate the occasional larger party.

You will be faced with finding the right balance between the table spacing — so that servers are able to work efficiently — and having the maximum number of seats to generate revenue. The traffic pattern has to be worked out: your guests must be easily able to access the washrooms and your servers must be able to serve and clear tables. You should do floor plans with several different table arrangements while you are working out the layout. Computer programs are available that can generate several mock-up plans once you have entered your dimensions and requirements. You can also make up floor plans to scale by using graph paper.

**KEY POINT:** Spend some time at your competition and observe the seating plan and how it works or doesn't work. Then incorporate the positive features into your layout.

## 6. A Word about Renovation

A renovation project can be both costly and time consuming, so it must be budgeted carefully in terms of material and labor costs, plus the downtime you will have while the renovation is underway. We have previously mentioned "fixed" costs — those costs that are incurred regardless of sales generated. These can be significant in a renovation project, so it is important that no avoidable delays be allowed to happen. The renovation must stay on schedule so that the door can open for business as soon as possible and you can start generating revenue.

Often a simple face-lift is required, and a designer can help you find a new look to reflect your style and concept. It may be as easy as changing the paint colors, adding some new lighting fixtures, replacing chairs, or changing linen colors and glassware. You may also want to add or create the feeling of warmth by bringing in some natural material, such as stone or wood, and adding personal touches as well. Pieces of art, antiques, and decorative fixtures can all contribute to placing your personal signature on your restaurant.

If structural changes are required, you will need to involve an architect and/or mechanical engineer to draw up the plans. A team approach usually works best, in which the designers and architect work together with you to develop the master plan. Once the plans have been approved, you must find a general contractor to bid on those plans and commit to a timetable for completing the work. The contractor will hire all the trades necessary to finish the total renovation, including the electrician, plumbers, carpenters, painters, masons, and any other workers required to complete the job to the specifications of your plan. If you are leasing the building, you will have to discuss the project with the building owner and see if he or she will contribute to any of the renovation costs.

*Design and renovation* **83**

# Chapter 8
# EQUIPMENT AND FURNISHINGS

Of course, no restaurant can open without the proper equipment and furnishings. But choosing these items can be complicated, and your choices will have long-term consequences. You'll find you constantly have to balance style with functionality, always keeping the future in mind.

## 1. Equipment

The equipment you'll need to operate an efficient kitchen will depend on your menu, restaurant size, and type of service. In other words, the questions you must ask yourself are, "What type of food do I plan to cook?"; "How many people am I cooking for?"; and "Am I serving the food at the table, over the counter (fast food), or for take out or delivery?" Your concept will dictate the menu and the style of service. The size of your establishment will determine the amounts of food you need to cook at any one time. If you are unsure about the equipment required to prepare your menu (although you should have researched this with your chef or a consulting chef as you developed your menu), by all means get some consulting advice. Sometimes it is possible simply to contract the chef or head cook you intend to hire to help you with menu and equipment decisions before he or she is needed full time.

To determine the size, make, and model of your kitchen equipment, we recommend that you review the manufacturer's specifications and select the piece of equipment that will handle your volume of business. Equipment sales representatives are also good sources of information and so are trade publications and manufacturers' Web sites.

Naturally, your equipment selection depends on several factors, function and cost being the two obvious ones. The availability and speed of service for that equipment must also be taken into account. There is little point in buying an expensive, state-of-the-art point-of-sale (POS) system (computerized cash/sales recording system), for example, if you cannot get an effective service contract. In our experience, POS systems break down — and sooner or later they all do — at 7:30 on a busy Friday night, not during business hours on a quiet Tuesday afternoon, when the equipment sales office is open. Having the appropriate, affordable repair service on call when you need it is an important consideration in any equipment purchase. Other considerations might be the time it takes to train staff to operate the equipment and the availability and cost of products needed in the operation of the equipment.

We remember some years ago when calculators with paper tape rolls were commonly used in offices. Some calculators were less than half the price of others and yet could perform the same functions. The catch was that the thermal paper tapes these calculators used were substantially more expensive and harder to find than regular paper tape rolls. It ended up costing more over a few years of standard usage to use the "half price" calculator than the ones with the higher purchase price. The moral of this story is simple: review all relevant costs (including consumables) before making the decision to buy a piece of equipment.

## 1.1 Sourcing equipment

Once you have developed your equipment list, you will need to source it. Hospitality magazines can provide a great deal of information about equipment. In Canada, check out *Foodservice and Hospitality* (phone 416-447-0888, or on the Web at <www.FoodserviceWorld.com>). In the United States, have a look at *Nation's Restaurant News* (phone 1-800-944-4676, or on the Web at <www.nrn.com>) or *Food Arts* (phone 212-684-4224). If you are set on purchasing a particular company's equipment, phone them and find out the name of their distributor or representative in your area. You can also do a search on the Internet using "food service equipment" as key words, and look for distributors and manufacturers in your area. The Web site <www.bestrestaurantequip.com/> is one example of a site providing information on equipment.

Another good source for information on equipment for sale is your newspaper's classified ads section. Auctions are also popular places to pick up used equipment.

## 1.2 New versus used equipment

Substantial savings can be had by making judicious purchases of used equipment. In most major urban centers there are plenty of restaurants closing, and sometimes you can find good deals. There are often second-hand dealers who specialize in purchasing used equipment for resale at bankruptcy auctions. Remember, however, that used equipment is often not guaranteed and *caveat emptor* (let the buyer beware) applies. Know what you're shopping for or take along someone who does.

Other than cost and servicing issues, there are two basic guidelines regarding purchasing used equipment:

(a) The less complicated a piece of equipment is, the more likely you are to get several more years of good use out of it.

(b) Equipment in the public eye needs to have that "new" look, while equipment for a closed kitchen or an office need only be functional.

**KEY POINT:** If you are going to buy used equipment, you will need someone to service it. Used equipment usually has a limited warranty or none at all. You must arrange for service. Cultivate a relationship with an independent repair person or local handyperson with appliance-repair skills — it can be a very valuable resource.

### 1.3 Buy versus lease equipment

Buying new or used equipment is, naturally, less expensive over time, but leasing can be an effective way of keeping down your start-up costs. Often certain suppliers can arrange very competitive lease contracts and will sometimes even loan equipment in exchange for guarantees to use their products. Two common examples are low-temperature chemical dishwashers/glass washers arranged by chemical detergent companies, and post- or pre-mix carbonated-beverage dispensers arranged by beverage suppliers.

Free use of a piece of equipment sounds great, but take a word of warning: in these cases, product exclusivity is usually required. That is, the company offering the equipment will likely say to you, "We can arrange an excellent lease deal on a post-mix carbonated-beverage dispenser for you, but you must agree to buy our beverage-syrup products and not to sell any other company's brand." But after a few years, you might like the ability to try another product, either due to customer demand or because the price of the products you are required to purchase has become too high. Your agreement to use the supplier's equipment might make it impossible for you to shop around. Before you sign any agreement, give careful consideration to all its advantages and disadvantages.

### 1.4 Kitchen equipment

The equipment you need for your kitchen depends on what you are going to cook and how you will cook it. Will you prepare your menu items à la minute" or will they be "held" in a steam-table waiting service? Will you use prepared products, or cook from scratch with fresh ingredients, or use some combination of the two? How big is your restaurant? How quickly do you intend to "turn" your tables? Your answers to these questions and many more like them will dictate the equipment you need. Your chef, your chef consultant, and your own experience cooking will help you determine the needs specific to your operation.

Equipment in a kitchen falls into three main areas:

(a) Storage and preparation

(b) The "hot line," for cooking and serving hot food

(c) The "cold station" (or *garde-manger*) for preparing and serving cold food

Storage usually involves refrigerated storage, freezer storage, and simple dry-good storage. Prep tables and prep sinks are placed near the storage area.

The hot line is a cooking bank made up of stoves, ovens, grills, deep fryers, and the like, depending on the type of menu to be prepared. The hot line may have a ventilation exhaust system or "hood" above it. Some kind of service-staff pick-up area, which may include a steam table, will face the cooking bank. The cold station is usually a preparation area with a reach-in refrigerator and/or freezer storage areas and a salad bar or similar cold pick-up area.

Of course, all equipment involved in direct service must be carefully positioned to allow the service staff to efficiently pick up plates to serve to the customers without getting in the way of one another or the cooking staff. Again, the facilities designer can help establish the optimum traffic flow.

## 1.5 Front-of-the-house equipment

In most cases the largest single expenditure for equipment is the computerized cash system, the "point of sale" (POS) system. The POS system is the heart of your cash and inventory control. There are many excellent systems on the market, and your decision on which to buy will depend on several factors. Virtually all systems will record all sales made and print them to individual guest checks. All the systems will separate sales by individual service staff. They will also summarize your sales in whatever categories you choose. For instance, all alcoholic beverages can be lumped together as "Total Beverage Sales." Or, for more discerning control, beverage sales could be subtotaled into categories such as "Liquor," "Wine," "Imported Bottled Beer," "Domestic Bottled Beer," "Imported Draught Beer," and "Domestic Draught Beer," depending on the amount of detailed sales information you wish to track.

The POS system can also calculate popularity indexes, which track the sales of all the menu items and compare them to each other and to the total sales figure. Some systems even deduct sales automatically from the appropriate inventories. How you use the various functions of a POS system depends on how you plan to use the information for control purposes (see chapter 13, "Cost Control") and to help with marketing and other decisions.

*Equipment and furnishings* **89**

A POS system has other advantages. The use of remote printers means service staff can place their orders with the bar or kitchen without having to go there in person. This allows large restaurants to minimize the time it takes to serve a table, as the service staff cover less distance when placing, picking up, and delivering orders. It also allows individual servers to more effectively serve large sections of the restaurant, therefore requiring fewer overall servers and saving payroll dollars. Some POS systems even allow for hand-held ordering keypads so the server can send the orders directly to the bar and kitchen while still at the tableside! A wonderful advantage for large restaurants, but perhaps not worth the extra investment for a small operation. Use Checklist 3, "POS System," to assess any POS system you are thinking of buying.

The bar is second only to the kitchen in concentration of equipment. Some restaurants have a stand-up or stool bar plus a service bar — a bar used to fill drinks placed only by the servers. If your restaurant has both, you will require equipment to serve drinks as well as produce them. Refrigeration for bottled beer and other beverages; draught taps and lines, and in some cases even the kegs themselves; sinks, glass washers, and glass-storage facilities; ice machines and ice service bins; and entertainment equipment (sound systems and televisions) are all commonly found behind the bar. Once again, exactly what you need and where it is placed will depend on many factors: restaurant size, style of service, and volume of sales are only a few.

## 2. Furnishings

Before opening your restaurant, you will need to decide on and budget for items such as the type of tables, chairs, lighting units, and pictures on the walls. A designer can be of assistance in this area, should you choose to use one. However, the following are a few general pointers that may help you with these decisions.

### 2.1 Tables

Though booths are more popular with customers, moveable, stand-alone tables allow for flexibility in seating. When deciding on the number and size of your tables, you must keep in mind the traffic flow around them. Sometimes it is wiser to choose small tables that can be easily put together for large parties. It is better to have to put two "deuces" together to seat a party of four than it is to sit two customers at a "quad" and lose two seats during a busy lunch.

# Checklist 3
# POS SYSTEM

Vendor Name: _____ Date: _____

Phone: _____ E-mail: _____ Fax: _____

Does the system have capability for the following functions? Bear in mind that these functions may not be required now, but you may need them as your operation grows.

|  | YES | NO |
|---|---|---|
| **General** | | |
| E-mail, Web, purchasing on-line | ❏ | ❏ |
| Desktop basic computer platforms | ❏ | ❏ |
| Payroll | ❏ | ❏ |
| Inventory control and purchasing | ❏ | ❏ |
| Connection from the front of house to kitchen | ❏ | ❏ |
| Multiple reservation lines | ❏ | ❏ |
| Generate customer receipts | ❏ | ❏ |
| Easy to learn and use | ❏ | ❏ |
| **Administrative reports** | | |
| Sales reports | | |
|     customer counts | ❏ | ❏ |
|     average check | ❏ | ❏ |
|     popularity index (sales mix) of menu items | ❏ | ❏ |
|     slow-moving items | ❏ | ❏ |
| Inventory lists | ❏ | ❏ |
| Server productivity | ❏ | ❏ |
| Food and beverage costing | ❏ | ❏ |

## Checklist 3 — Continued

|  | YES | NO |
|---|---|---|
| **Customer database** |  |  |
| Customer profiling | ❏ | ❏ |
| Customer sign-up for frequent dining benefits | ❏ | ❏ |
| Mailing lists for customer birthdays | ❏ | ❏ |
| Customized customer come-back coupon or other promotional material on customer receipt | ❏ | ❏ |
| **Does the company from which you will purchase your POS system do the following?** |  |  |
| Take responsibility for the system once it is installed | ❏ | ❏ |
| Provide cell, beeper numbers for technicians | ❏ | ❏ |
| Give references (other restaurants using the system) | ❏ | ❏ |
| State its length of time in business | ❏ | ❏ |
| Provide installation assistance | ❏ | ❏ |
| Provide training assistance | ❏ | ❏ |
| Have a maintenance program | ❏ | ❏ |

Naturally, tables, like any other furnishing, must fit the look and feel of the room — but don't pay a lot of money for wonderful marble or wood-finished tabletops if you plan on covering the tops with table clothes anyway! Many very exclusive fine-dining restaurants use lovely tablecloths over simple plywood tabletops that their customers never see.

If your floor coverings are irregular — flagstone or various types of ceramic tile for example — make sure your tables have adjustable legs to prevent the dreaded "rocking table" syndrome that frustrated customers end up sticking matchbooks under table legs to remedy. Similarly, tables with built-in glides will prevent the table feet from scratching or damaging a beautiful floor finish.

## 2.2 Chairs

Your choice of a style of chair depends on many factors: look, sturdiness, cost, and ability to repair or replace are all considerations. Sometimes booths or banquettes will allow for a better use of seating space against a wall. Other factors also come into play; for example, the standard 18-inch chair seat is more often not quite large enough these days for an aging modern North American market!

As with tables, attaching glides to the chair feet will protect fine floor finishes as well as allow for easier, quieter use. When selecting chairs with fabric-covered padding, consider the problems of durability and cleaning.

## 2.3 Other furnishings

Other necessary furniture may include sideboards, bus stations, and bar and back-bar pieces. Carefully review the functionality of all furniture as well as how it fits into the overall design concept. Both functionality and fit can differ drastically depending on the type and style of your restaurant. Always be true to your own vision.

## 2.4 Kitchen/bar small wares

Small wares usually include all the cooking utensils, pots, pans, and other serving utensils. Once again, the specifics of the initial purchase will depend on the type of food you plan to serve, how you will be preparing it, and the individual preferences of you or your chef.

*Equipment and furnishings* **93**

For instance, if your menu has stir-fried items, you may need a vertical blender such as the Vita-Prep or a vertical chopping machine (VCM), which operates on the same principal as a blender. Or if you are having to prep a large volume of vegetables that require shredding, dicing, and slicing, you will want to look at the different types of food processors and buffalo choppers available. If your signature item is a "house smoked" or cured item, a small smoker would be in order. A pasta maker would be a good idea if you a featuring "homemade" noodles on your menu. An electric meat slicer or hand-held mandoline may or may not be necessary depending on your menu. For desserts made in house, you may require ice-cream machines or special equipment for tempering chocolate. You may also need a heavy-duty mixer if you are baking on the premises. If you are preparing foie gras or pâtés in house, you will need to invest in terrine molds.

Your chef should be given a budget to purchase small wares for the kitchen to facilitate menu preparation. Items such as sheet pans, wire cooling racks, and rolling storage racks for the sheet pans are all necessary, but quantities will vary depending on the amount of production that you are doing in house versus outsourcing. Your pot-and-pan selection will also depend on your menu and the quantities of sauce that you prepare — will you be making stocks and sauces or purchasing them in paste form? Whips, ladles, and spoons come in various sizes and weights depending on their intended use, so once again, while these items will be necessary for sauce making and service, the quantities and sizes will be specific to your operation. Some chefs like to use "squeeze" bottles for cold sauces or dressings instead of spooning the sauces onto the plate.

Small wares tend to go missing, and may need to be stored in a locked area if this becomes an issue.

**KEY POINT:** You should take a small-wares inventory at least quarterly to keep an accurate account of these items. Perhaps reward your kitchen staff with some meaningful incentive if no items have gone missing.

If you are not the chef, then consult him or her before making these purchases. There are a great number of elaborate kitchen "gizmos" on the market that restaurant supply dealers love to sell, and a professional cook will have little use for many of them. Buy only what you really need. The same applies to the bar, which we will cover in more detail in chapter 14, "Bars and Pubs."

For a list of items you may need for your kitchen, see Sample 4.

**KEY POINT:** Your chef and kitchen staff will have some of their own small equipment, such as knives and specialty tools and items they have collected over time. They will need an area to safely store their tool boxes, and they should be encouraged to have their names or identifying mark on the handles to avoid loss.

## 2.5 Dinnerware (china, flatware, glassware, linen)

Like furniture, the decision on the purchase of these chattels is dependent on the type, concept, and style of service of the individual restaurant. The "look," or how they fit into the overall concept, is the most important element to consider in the decision about what to purchase. Unlike furniture, however, durability and the ability to be replaced are of the greatest importance. Remember that you will constantly be losing these items to breakage and theft, and sometimes at a much higher rate then you might anticipate. (The Holiday Inn hotel chain proclaimed a few years ago that they lost a towel to theft every 11 seconds.)

Decisions about these products are fraught with other problems, too. As co-author Brian Floody says, "It always seemed to me that no sooner did I purchase an inventory of a new style of china or glassware than the manufacturer of the product would double the price, or decide to stop producing that particular line, or go bankrupt!"

Before you purchase your dinnerware, consider the folllowing factors. Can you answer these questions?

- *Style:* Does it suit your restaurant?
- *Initial cost:* Can you afford the style you like?
- *Durability:* Will they last through constant handling and washings?

## Sample 4
# KITCHEN SMALL WARES

Most of the items listed here will be useful in all kitchens, but the quantities and sizes you'll need will be influenced by many factors, including your menu, style of cooking, kitchen size, storage area, and budget. If your kitchen is open to the restaurant, the equipment becomes part of the "show" and may therefore affect your materials selection; for instance, copper may be used to enhance the image or may be perceived as added value.

**Measuring Equipment and General Items Used for Preparation**

- Stainless steel mixing bowls (various sizes, depending on volume of production)
- Graduated measuring pitchers and cups for measuring liquids
- Measuring spoons
- Scales for weighing ingredients for portion control (spring, balance, or electronic)
- Whips/whisks
- Sieves, strainers, and chinoise for sifting dry ingredients and for straining cooked or puréed foods
- Fine cheesecloth for straining
- Colanders (various sizes)
- Rotary or swivel-blade peeler for peeling skin from fruits and vegetables
- Pastry bags and various tips for piping out puréed food and toppings
- Slotted and solid metal spoons
- Stainless steel tongs (various lengths)
- Kitchen forks for turning meats
- Wooden spoons
- Skimmers for skimming stocks and sauces
- Spatulas (offset, for turning foods; rubber, for scraping)
- Can opener for #10 cans
- Storage containers to hold food safely in both refrigerator and freezers. (These may be plastic or stainless steel with lids. You should have tools for marking the item and date on the containers — markers and tape.)
- Vegetable juicer

## Sample 4 — Continued

**Pots and Pans**

You will have several materials to choose from when selecting pots. Pots and pans are made from copper, cast iron, stainless steel, black steel, blue steel, and aluminum. The surface may also have a nonstick coating. The main guidelines to follow when making your selections are to choose sizes appropriate for the food being cooked and to choose material appropriate to the cooking techniques being used.

- Stockpot (Marmite; some have a spigot at the base for ease of straining)
- Saucepot (various sizes)
- Rondeau for braising
- Sauteuse or sauté pan
- Sautoir for pan frying
- Omelet pan
- Grill pan
- Roasting pans
- Bain-Marie or double boiler
- Sheet pans, full or half-size, for baking and traying up items
- Hotel pan for holding foods that are already cooked in steamtables, hot boxes, or steamers

**Knives**

- French knives
- Paring knives
- Utility knife
- Boning knives
- Slicer
- Cleaver
- Sharpening stone

(It's your call as to whether you will provide these basic knives or your staff must provide their own. Usually the chef will have his or her own set of knives, but your prep people may not, so a basic set should be available for their use.)

☞ *Replacement cost:* Can you afford to keep sufficient inventory on hand?

☞ *Availability:* Will the manufacturers of the line of china, glassware, etc., you choose still be around when you need a replacement order? If they are based outside the country, will their supplier or agent be available?

A competent restaurant-supply dealer can answer many of the above questions. Dealers can be very helpful, and establishing a relationship with a good one can ensure you good advice and good service over the years. But even well-respected dealers cannot be expected to be completely objective, so shop around.

In the case of linens, some of these problems can be circumvented. Linens can often be rented from a linen service, as can kitchen uniforms, bar towels, and the like. But be careful, as these services can be expensive.

### 2.5a  How much should you purchase initially?

How much china, glassware, or flatware you need depends to some degree on the number of different varieties of plates, bowls, cups, and glasses that you plan to use. As a general rule, when designing the presentation of your menu items, try to minimize the number of different types of dishes involved.

Take glassware at the bar as an example. Don't overlook the merchandizing value of eye-pleasing glassware, but, if possible, use the same type of glass to serve various different cocktails. Obviously you cannot put a screwdriver in the same glass as a martini. But screwdrivers, Bloody Marys, rye and ginger, rum and coke, and similar "built" drinks can all go in a standard eight- to ten-ounce highball glass. If you try to use a specialty glass for every drink, you will end up with far too large a variety of glasses. You must then train all your staff to use each type of glass appropriately. You will also have to find storage behind the bar for your large selection of glasses. Your poor bartenders will inevitably be tearing their hair out, screaming at the bussers, trying to find just the right glass for a certain cocktail when there has been an inexplicable run on just those particular cocktails during the busiest lunch of the year!

The busier the bar, the fewer types of glasses should be used. If you have a service bar for a small fine-dining restaurant in which dining is

**98**  *Start and run a restaurant business*

leisurely, a series of elegant glasses for several different types of cocktails will work just fine (provided you have the storage space). But for a larger, busier operation, less variety of glassware is better. The same applies to dinner plates, side plates, and dessert dishes.

This still leaves us with the question of how large an inventory you need to get started — a difficult question to answer, as the number of each item depends on the style of restaurant and the tastes of the target market. Naturally, a fine-dining restaurant will need more wineglasses than beer glasses, and the exact opposite will be true for a pub.

Business volume usually builds up gradually, and you can start with about the same number of plates, side plates, cups, saucers, knives, and forks as you have seats. However, you will need one-and-a-half times your number of seats for coffee/tea spoons, as they are in greater usage, and much less of specialty glassware — perhaps less than a case of each will do depending on the restaurant's size and the number of drinks each type of glass is supporting. This will usually do to start, as long as you can order and receive more without delay as your business grows.

**KEY POINT:** If you are having a large kick-off party on opening day — which we do *not* recommend — use rented china, glassware, and flatware to accommodate the large turnout. However, we feel it is better to have a "soft" opening — that is, an opening day to which you invite family and friends; one that allows you and your staff to work out the kinks and glitches on a smaller crowd. Then, after you are satisfied that your kitchen and service staff can handle the volume (and that you have the right equipment and amount of dinnerware!), plan the large kick-off party to create some excitement.

## Chapter 9
# YOUR EMPLOYEES

The heart and soul of any hospitality business are its employees. On one hand, the best-tasting meal served in the loveliest setting can turn to sawdust in your mouth if served by arrogant or surly table staff. On the other hand, a cheery, friendly server can charm you into happily accepting minor delays or feeling good when a mistaken order is replaced with an apology and a smile. Every major customer survey shows the same thing: what customers want most is good service — more than beautiful surroundings, often even more than good food!

We will discuss the art of service at some length in chapter 11, but the essence of good service is great attitude — and that is hard to find and even harder (some say impossible) to teach. When hiring employees, great attitude is what you must look for: the desire to do the best possible job, an eagerness to learn and to succeed, a generally cheery disposition. These are the character traits for which every good employer searches. Skills can be taught much more easily than attitude; hire people that already have it.

# 1. Job Analysis, Job Description, and Job Specifications

As discussed in the opening chapters of this book, it is crucial to surround yourself with staff members who complement you or your partners' individual talents. If you yourself are an outstanding culinarian, you would probably not need to hire a chef as a key member of your opening operation team. If, however, you are a front-of-the-house specialist, the acquisition of a chef might well be your first priority before you design your menu and kitchen.

When hiring someone to do a job, you must first analyze the job itself, and this means writing out as extensive a job description as you can. For example, what exactly do you expect an executive chef to do? See Sample 5, "Job Description," for an idea of what you should include. The more precise you are with the written job description, the better your chances of finding just the right person for the job.

Once you have done your job analyses and have written out your job descriptions, you can decide on each job's specifications. Job specifications are the skills, knowledge, and experience you decide a candidate must have to be able to successfully start the job. Job specifications usually form part of an advertisement for prospective job candidates. Be careful here, however. You do not want the job specifications to be any more onerous then they need to be! See Sample 6, "Job Specifications," for an example.

A client who consulted co-author Brian Floody some years ago complained bitterly that he could seldom find dishwashers, and when he did, they never lasted very long. When asked what his job specifications for this position were, he replied that he asked for minimal experience but he did want job applicants to have successfully completed high school. When Brian asked him how the completion of high school would make someone a better dishwasher, the restaurateur could not answer. Perhaps many a potentially excellent dishwasher had not even bothered to apply. The bar had been set higher than necessary and had become a deterrent to applicants who may have had all the knowledge, abilities, and attitude needed to do a great job. When the employer took the high school requirement out of his job specifications, he found he attracted many more candidates with much better working attitudes. These people usually lasted substantially longer in the job, too, because they were better suited to it.

**102**  *Start and run a restaurant business*

## *Sample 5*
# JOB DESCRIPTION

**Title:** Executive Chef

**Reports to:** Owner

**Responsibilities:**
- Plans menus, including plate presentations
- Develops signature dishes
- Purchases food items
- Ensures quality control
- Participates in setting the food and beverage budget; is responsible for food and labor cost control
- Sets specifications for all food products
- Hires, trains, and evaluates staff
- Creates schedules for kitchen staff
- Maintains open communication with front-of-house manager and wait staff
- Coordinates special events and promotions

## Sample 6
## JOB SPECIFICATIONS

**Job:** Executive Chef

**Education:** Graduate of a 2-year culinary arts program

**Experience:** Minimum 5 years' experience working in a senior-level culinary position. Will have examples of menus that he/she has created and demonstrate cooking ability by way of menu sampling/tasting. Must have knowledge of Thai cuisine, be creative, and have excellent communication skills.

In putting together job specifications, make certain the specifications you assign to each job are essential only to the job itself. Keep the pool of potential candidates as large as possible.

## 2. Recruitment

When you begin the hiring process, your success in finding the right people to help you run your restaurant depends on where you advertise for employees. The wider you can cast your net when searching for candidates, the likelier you are to find the best person for the job. Be especially careful with your key positions. General managers, assistant managers, and chefs or head cooks are critical positions, and getting the best people you can will make all the difference in the successful opening and operation of your restaurant.

When seeking candidates for any position in your restaurant, advertise as widely as you can to as many groups in society as are suitable. Use conventional print media when it will reach a wide audience, but don't forget smaller community newspapers, calls to the placement offices of local hospitality schools, or even the use of flyers, posters, word of mouth, or the old-fashioned sign in the window.

In addition, when recruiting, don't ignore groups of people that might be very suitable for the position but who are often overlooked because they have not traditionally been seen in these jobs. Women and the elderly are often not considered for jobs in certain areas of the hospitality industry, when in fact they can make the best employees. Many people with so called "handicaps" can be just as competent as anyone else in most jobs. Remember: You are looking for attitude, first and foremost.

A good ad should include a brief description of the type of restaurant you are operating and the meals periods that will be served. You must also include a phone number to which candidates can reply. Sample 7, "Job Ad," shows a commonly used format for a restaurant-position employment ad.

# 3. *Selection*

Once you have attracted as many people with the basic qualifications as possible, it is finally time to begin to choose who will fill the position available.

The most common tools used to assist in the selection process are:

(a) The completed application form and/or résumé. Think about designing your own job-specific application forms to help you gather as much pertinent information as possible.

(b) The references, which should be carefully checked.

(c) Information from previous employers and/or past fellow employees, who should be questioned when possible.

(d) The interview(s), during which you should ask open-ended, leading questions and let the candidate do most of the talking.

(e) The new hire's performance on the job and his or her ability to relate to customers, management, and fellow employees during a probationary work period.

Key personnel should be hired first. The chef is commonly taken on early enough to help develop the menu and oversee any kitchen renovation and equipment and small-wares purchasing, as well as the hiring of the kitchen staff.

You may want to have candidates for the management positions send in résumés so that you can screen these prior to setting up interviews. However, when dealing with candidates for general employment, it is a good idea to have them come in and fill out an application form in person and speak to you or a manager at that time. The key personnel from each area — kitchen and front of the house — can help do

## Sample 7
## JOB AD

**Executive Chef**

Executive Chef needed to create signature dishes, mentor a team of cooks, for our 75-seat, dinner-only bistro, located in Yourtown. This position is a platform for showcasing your culinary talents, fiscal responsibility, and creativity. Interested chefs call 555-1234 between 12:00 noon and 3:00 p.m. to schedule your menu/cooking presentation.

the initial interviewing. This is essential when hiring an initial group of employees for a new restaurant. The so-called "paper selection" — the screening of résumés, by which applicants who do not even meet the basic job specifications are rejected — can be eliminated for line-level staff. Doing so will allow you to gain a first impression of a prospective employee's demeanor and attitude. Occasionally, this technique also allows you to meet and assess candidates whose paper application might have been rejected due to poor writing skills. By talking to them directly, you may discover they have the skills you seek. You can use Checklist 4 to assist you in your hiring and interviewing.

When hiring a large group of employees at the beginning of a new restaurant venture, it can be a good idea to set up an "application day" or days on which you and your key employees meet job candidates. However, do not hire up to capacity before you open. Once the word spreads that a new restaurant is open, some potentially excellent employees might wander in to "check the place out." Leave a little room in the initial hiring to take advantage of any late-rising stars.

A high turnover rate is all too common in the hospitality industry. Too often restaurant staff are hired quickly with little thought or effort because they are required immediately. Existing staff are asked if they "know anyone who needs work." Sometimes good employees are found this way, but in our experience, only rarely. Don't let your management fall into this vicious circle of poor hiring practices. There is a high cost

## Checklist 4
# HIRING/INTERVIEW CHECKLIST

**NAME** _____ **DATE** _____

**POSITION SOUGHT** _____

**INTERVIEWED BY** _____

### Qualifications/Abilities

Relevant restaurant experience ❑
Culinary degree (or other) ❑
Proficiency in skill required ❑
Demonstrated knowledge of food and wine ❑
Provided references ❑

### Characteristics

Positive attitude ❑
Neat in appearance ❑
Made eye contact/polite ❑
Spoke clearly (if applicable) ❑
Willing to learn and work with others ❑

### Notes/Observations

_____

_____

### Recommendation

❑ Outstanding  ❑ High potential  ❑ Satisfactory  ❑ Not Suitable

107

to constantly hiring and training new, poorly selected staff, who will not last long anyway, because they do not really suit the jobs for which they were hired.

## 4. Orientation and Training

Once you have decided whom to hire, you must follow up with proper orientation and initial training. An orientation package should be prepared for the new hire that should include:

(a) A written introduction to you and your company. What do you stand for? What is your mission statement? Describe your dream to them. After all, you want them to share it!

(b) A copy of any policies from the house policy and procedures manual that affect the employee's position. Include a description of the values that the employee is expected to demonstrate, such as honesty, diligence, punctuality, and teamwork. You must build a culture of teamwork and honesty among your staff, and it starts right here, during each employee's training period.

(c) A written job description of the position, including a list of the specific tasks that the employee is expected to perform.

(d) Floor plans, menus, and any other material that will help the new employee get to know the operation and feel at home as quickly as possible.

(e) All legal forms: agreements regarding payroll, employee deductions, employee benefits, required government forms, insurance releases.

The orientation session(s) should follow. Several points should be covered. See Checklist 5, "Orientation Procedures," for a list of the most important ones.

Formal training for the job should take place under the direction of the appropriate supervisor or designated training staff. The use of trainer and trainee checklists is valuable; see Checklist 6, "Floor Training Checklist," for an example of a format that can be adapted to other positions. Checklists ensure that all new trainees are given all the information and practice necessary to enable them to do the job on their own.

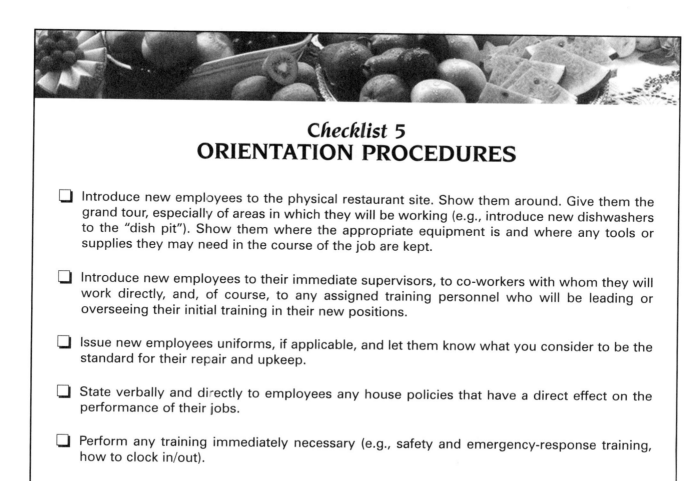

Many restaurateurs organize ongoing tests on house policies and procedures as part of the orientation process. Individuals who perform well on these written and practical tests are given promotions, raises, or prizes to reward their success.

## 5. Policy and Procedure Manuals

The creation of a complete policy and procedure manual is an enormous task and must always be viewed as a work in progress. It would be completely unrealistic — and indeed foolish — to attempt to write a complete manual for your restaurant before you open. Many policies and procedures grow out of the trial and error of the first few months of operation, and all must be continually updated to meet the ever-changing needs of the customers and the staff.

## Checklist 6
# FLOOR TRAINING CHECKLIST

**Employee's name:** _____

### General

Management has provided the following to the new employee:

| | |
|---|---|
| Job description | ☐ |
| Schedule | ☐ |
| Floor-staff duty sheet | ☐ |
| Table numbers/floor diagram | ☐ |
| House policy manual | ☐ |

### Human Resources

Employee has provided the following to management:

| | |
|---|---|
| Social insurance or social security number | ☐ |
| Address and phone number | ☐ |

### Three-Day Training Checklist

Employee is given instruction and training on the following:

*Front-of-house operation:*

| | Day 1 | Day 2 | Day 3 |
|---|---|---|---|
| POS system | ☐ | ☐ | ☐ |
| Menu selection/wine-pairing information | ☐ | ☐ | ☐ |
| Coffee/espresso machine | ☐ | ☐ | ☐ |
| Glass washer | ☐ | ☐ | ☐ |
| Ordering and picking up beverages | ☐ | ☐ | ☐ |
| Ordering and picking up food | ☐ | ☐ | ☐ |
| Bussing duties | ☐ | ☐ | ☐ |

# Checklist 6 — Continued

|  | Day 1 | Day 2 | Day 3 |
|---|---|---|---|
| *Opening duties:* | | | |
| Table set-up | ☐ | ☐ | ☐ |
| Side duties | ☐ | ☐ | ☐ |
| Ashtrays | ☐ | ☐ | ☐ |
| Salt and pepper refills | ☐ | ☐ | ☐ |
| Coffee station | ☐ | ☐ | ☐ |
| Glassware | ☐ | ☐ | ☐ |
| Silverware | ☐ | ☐ | ☐ |
| Sign in | ☐ | ☐ | ☐ |
| Guest checks | ☐ | ☐ | ☐ |
| *Closing duties:* | | | |
| Station duties/clean up | ☐ | ☐ | ☐ |
| Cash out | ☐ | ☐ | ☐ |
| Sign out | ☐ | ☐ | ☐ |

**Manager's Comments**

_____

_____

_____

Date _____

However, you do need the skeleton of a policy and procedure manual in place as you begin to train your staff. A description of the tasks involved in each position (wait staff, bartender, prep cook, etc.) should be written up by the supervisor for each area. These job descriptions must be specific to your own operation, detailing step by step what is expected of the employees during their shifts. Primary duties, secondary duties, and any other responsibilities must be spelled out. The better employees understand what is expected of them, the better they will perform.

Many other rules must be laid out in the manuals as well: emergency procedures, payroll procedures, general dos and don'ts, as well as things such as where and when the staff are allowed to eat or what music should be played when and at what volume level. All of these details should first be sketched out by the supervisors of each area, with input from you. Take some care with the general policy dos and don'ts. They should reflect your own basic philosophy and grow out of your mission statement and/or your basic concept. The heart and soul of your dream are embodied in these policies and procedures, just as much as they are in the look of your restaurant and the taste of your food.

## 6. *Reward and Discipline*

It must be made clear to all employees from the very first what is expected of them and what they can expect in return. Employees must know how they are expected to perform; how much and when they will be paid; and how they can earn bonuses, raises, and promotion. They must also understand the consequences of poor performance, dereliction of duty, and dishonesty. As a business owner, you should endeavor to treat people fairly and equitably. Most important, lead by example! People will always understand and respond to "Do as I do," but they will rarely perform well in a climate of "Do as I say, not as I do."

You must embody the passion of your own dream. Your staff will never be able to perform at the level you expect unless they see that standard reflected in you every day. For example, if one of your policies for all employees is no eating from the cooking line, then it would be very inappropriate for you, the owner, to go into the kitchen and eat shrimps — or anything else — from the work stations or line. The same goes for any behavior that is strictly forbidden for your staff. Drinking at the bar after hours is often a policy issue, and if your policy is that no employees are allowed to do so, the rule must be enforced unilaterally, and consequences for abusing it should be well known to all staff.

One of the partners in co-author Brian Cooper's Italian Restaurant chain enjoyed providing his friends with free rounds of drinks when they visited the restaurant. He felt that as he was an owner/partner, he was entitled to the fruits of his labor. Brian, however, after several months of noting the difficulty the restaurant had in meeting the required potential beverage cost, observed the managers and senior staff providing drinks for the regular staff who frequented the restaurant. When Brian confronted the staff, he was informed that the staff were merely following the example of the partner who took great pleasure in providing rounds of drinks. The partner and staff were told that in future they would invoice all freebie drinks on a guest check and have them approved by Brian Cooper on his next visit. The number of free rounds declined immediately, and the beverage cost came into line.

# 7. *Performance Appraisals*

At least once a year, sit down with each of your employees and constructively discuss their performance with regard to your expectations, and also your performance with regard to their expectations. Do they feel appreciated in their work? Which aspects of their performance can be improved? Would they like to be trained for other positions? Moving employees up through your internal job strata to management is an excellent way to develop good, trustworthy managers. Set goals and time lines for improvement, and give praise and rewards where warranted. Do not link raises directly to the performance appraisal, but always to actual increases in responsibility.

One way of simplifying performance appraisals is to establish a form (see Sample 8, "Performance Appraisal") and then perform the following steps:

(a) Fill out the appraisal form before meeting with the employee to discuss his or her performance. Have the employee fill out the form in advance as well. You will be amazed by how well employees recognize their own weaknesses and strengths if you ask them to do a self-appraisal before the meeting. This leads to a very productive interview.

(b) Discuss the questions at the performance appraisal meeting itself, giving particular attention to any discrepancies between the two forms. Employees will often be harder on themselves than management will!

(c) Set time lines for measurable performance improvement, if needed, and always follow up on those time lines with appropriate performance checks and further discussion. This is often the missing link of performance appraisals. Failure to follow up leads employees to believe that management doesn't really care.

A performance appraisal should always be done in a positive, constructive way! Never use the performance appraisal simply to reprimand without a plan for improving performance. If the employee walks away from the meeting discouraged and with no ray of hope, the appraisal will do more harm than good.

## 8. Pay Scales

How do you know what to pay your staff? If you are not acquainted with the going rates of pay, do a little research. Ask people working in other restaurants in the area. If you have already hired some of your key personnel, they will probably have a good idea of the local pay scales. Talk to hospitality employment agencies. Check with your local hospitality business associations. You can also check the Internet. Legal requirements such as minimum wage rates and other employment standards are often posted on government and business-related Web sites. In the United States, try <www.toolkit.cch.com/text/P05_4029.asp>. In Canada, try <www.hrsdc.gc.ca>.

## 9. Management Communications

Good communication is essential to the smooth operation of any restaurant. Communicating to your managers and employees your vision of how your restaurant should operate is an ongoing task and must be facilitated in every way possible.

Owners must effectively communicate with their managers. Managers must constantly communicate with each other and with their employees. Employees must communicate with each other. In short, all are part of a team, and successful teams are ones that communicate well among themselves.

## Sample 8
# PERFORMANCE APPRAISAL

Performance appraisal forms should be given to the employee three days before the actual appraisal meeting is scheduled. The employee will complete and bring it to the meeting.

Employee's name: _____

Position/title: _____

Date of hire: _____ Date of evaluation: _____

Type of evaluation: _____Probation _____Annual _____Other

---

The objective of a performance evaluation is to provide an opportunity for the employee and his/her supervisor to review the employee's performance, to examine both strengths and weaknesses, and to discuss future goals and development strategies.

I have read and understood this appraisal:

Employee's signature: _____ Date: _____

Supervisor's signature: _____ Date: _____

Supervisor's position: _____

# Sample 8 — Continued

| FACTORS | DESCRIPTION | RATING | | | | |
|---|---|---|---|---|---|---|
| | | 1. | 2. | 3. | 4. | 5. |
| Reliability | Punctuality and attendance | ❏ | ❏ | ❏ | ❏ | ❏ |
| Knowledge of job | Understands responsibilities and duties related to the position | ❏ | ❏ | ❏ | ❏ | ❏ |
| Skill level | Level at which the employee is currently working | ❏ | ❏ | ❏ | ❏ | ❏ |
| Productivity | Quality of work: accuracy, presentation Quantity of work: speed and efficiency; working to set standards within time limits | ❏ | ❏ | ❏ | ❏ | ❏ |
| Organizational ability | Establishes appropriate priorities in completing workload and is able to adjust those priorities when necessary | ❏ | ❏ | ❏ | ❏ | ❏ |
| Working relationships | With peers, associates, managers Willingness and ability to work with others to ensure work is completed | ❏ | ❏ | ❏ | ❏ | ❏ |
| Food handling/ sanitation/safety | Follows proper food handling and safety procedures | ❏ | ❏ | ❏ | ❏ | ❏ |
| Personal care | Grooming, dress, health, cleanliness | ❏ | ❏ | ❏ | ❏ | ❏ |

## Rating Scale

1. Unsatisfactory performance (below the acceptable standard)

2. Needs improvement  (not performing at the level demanded by the position)

3. Average performance (working at the acceptable standard for the position)

4. Above-average performance (excellent command of the position; skill level above standard)

5. Exceptional performance (outstanding performance and delivery of all aspects of the position)

## Sample 8 — Continued

**COMMENTS**

Employee's best qualities:
_____
_____

In what areas can improvement be made?
_____
_____

**GOALS**
_____
_____

Steps that will be taken to achieve these goals:

1.

2.

3.

**OVERALL PERFORMANCE RATING (Check one item only)**

| | |
|---|---|
| Unsatisfactory | ❏ |
| Needs improvement | ❏ |
| Average | ❏ |
| Above average | ❏ |
| Exceptional | ❏ |

## 9.1 Log books and incident and accident reports

It is far more difficult than you might imagine to be sure that important information is passed on to managers who will be working successive shifts. Simple information, such as an employee phoning in sick or equipment that is broken and must be repaired, is vitally important to the manager working a subsequent shift. He or she must be made aware of anything that might impact the smooth operation of the restaurant. It is far too easy for a day manager just finishing a shift to forget to tell the night manager some important piece of information during the busy time of "shift changeover." A good way to ensure this does not happen is the use of the old marine protocol of the log book. Just as the officer of the watch wrote in the log book any pertinent information about events that happened during their watch, so too the manager on duty (MOD) should document any events or pertinent information in the managers' log book. Doing so allows the managers working the subsequent shifts to be prepared for any difficulties that might arise from that information.

Any information that comes to light that might impact the smooth operation of the restaurant in the present or in the future should be recorded. Better to write too much than too little. Many operations use specific incident and/or accident report forms that detail the kind of information that should be recorded if an accident, fire, robbery, or other disruptive event takes place. When an incident that might have important future legal or other implications occurs, there is certain information that must be recorded. This usually includes the old "four Ws and an H" of basic journalism: Who, What, Where, When, and How. If the incident might involve insurance or litigation, the Who should include the name and contact information of any witnesses as well as the principals of the event. Any significant events should also be reviewed by the full management team at the next managers' meeting.

## 9.2 Managers' meetings

One common obstacle to good communication among the management team and between management and staff is the problem of "When can we meet to talk about things?" Many restaurants are open seven days a week for lunch and dinner, and therefore some staff and management are always working, making it difficult to schedule information meetings that all of the staff can attend. Even so, having regularly scheduled staff and management meetings is still the best way to communicate new information and to review the restaurant's ongoing operation. The management team should meet weekly, and full staff meetings should be held monthly or quarterly at the minimum. These meetings should have a written agenda, and minutes should be kept and distributed to all participants afterward. See Sample 9, "Meeting Agenda."

**KEY POINT:** A valuable technique you might consider to keep managers from getting bored of the meeting routine is to rotate the chairing of the meetings. Each manager takes a turn organizing the information for the meetings from the various log books and incident reports. This strategy prevents you or the general manager from appearing to dominate the agenda or from appearing simply to pontificate on a weekly basis.

## Sample 9
# MEETING AGENDA

1. The meeting is brought to order

2. Attendance is taken

3. Review of last meeting's minutes

4. Review of any information that is being "tracked" (kept track of on a weekly basis to observe growth or change)

    For example:

    - the past week's sales and/or costs versus budgeted sales and/or cost targets
    - the past week's sales versus sales for the same period last year
    - customer complaints or comment cards
    - the number of tickets sold for an upcoming promotion
    - the number of coupons redeemed from a given advertisement

    or any other information you wish to track weekly.

5. Review any needed repairs or maintenance required (or in progress)

6. Review any staff issues, such as discipline problems or new trainees' progress

7. Update on preparations for upcoming private parties, banquets, or promotional events and/or review or post-mortem any recent events to determine if they went as planned or if changes should be made for the next time

8. General comments or updating of all managers regarding any events that might impact the day-to-day business of the restaurant over the next week

9. Adjournment

# Part 3
# MANAGING YOUR OPERATION

The doors will soon be opened, and initial horror stories can now be repeated with laughter and new-found confidence. It's time to finalize your menu and decide on the type of service that best suits your concept. At last you can begin to hire and train that "dream team" of employees you planned for, who will introduce your concept to the public. Rarely does everything go easily before opening day, though. The carpet is laid down only the night before, and the health and liquor inspectors haven't arrived yet with their approval stamps. You and your partners are in a daze while potential customers line up to give you their opinions. And this is only the beginning!

Part 3 takes you through marketing your new business and developing the food, beverage, and labor controls that will suit your operation. Good luck!

# *Chapter* 10
# YOUR MENU

As discussed in chapter 1, "Before You Start," your restaurant concept is defined by and embodied in your menu. The menu you create will greatly influence your choice of location, décor, marketing plan, the types of customers you wish to attract, and the employees that you hire. The menu is your restaurant's signature and it will continue to evolve, just as your operation will. The food is the star in most restaurants and is the main reason for a customer to choose your restaurant. You will want to create a menu that evokes a sense of adventure or indulgence and yet reflects the concept and culture of your establishment.

However, any new restaurateur would do well to bear in mind Brian Cooper's word of warning from chapter 1: Place items on the menu only that are within your own capacity to prepare. Another suggestion would be to have your number 2 in the kitchen, your sous-chef, able to prepare all the items on the menu in case of an emergency situation.

This chapter will discuss types of menus, menu pricing, menu layout and presentation, and developing your wine list. Be creative and have fun!

# 1. Types of Menus

Your menu may feature a combination of any of these types of menus:

☞ *À la carte*: each menu item is priced separately.

☞ *Prix fixe*: set menu for a fixed price; this concept has evolved into the "meal deal" or "combo," standard in fast-food outlets.

☞ *Table d'hôte*: also a set menu for an inclusive price, but you may offer some choice within the menu selection — perhaps a choice of three entrées or two appetizers.

☞ *Menu degustation*: the chef's tasting menu. It can feature anywhere from 5 to 12 courses at a price that is higher than a three-course meal. Some restaurants will offer a tasting menu in addition to their à la carte menu, but the tasting menu can also be the only menu offered. At Charlie Trotter's in Chicago, a guest is offered three choices of menu degustation: the grand menu; the vegetable menu; and the kitchen-table menu, with its amazing 15 courses.

☞ *Amuse bouche*: a "mouth pleaser" — tasty, bite-size portions of the chef's creation. This is given to guests at some restaurants to excite their palates. Amuse bouche has long been part of the classic French menu and is now finding its way into the mainstream. Guests love the indulgence and the attention that this "extra" supplies. Providing amuse bouche may also set you apart from your competition.

These terms have their roots in classic French cuisine. Today it's not uncommon to see a menu that utilizes several different structures. The most familiar type of menu is one on which each item is priced separately. However, you may also see a combining of appetizer and dessert with the main course in a set menu offering; this is a way to increase your average check. Set menus also work well for special holiday menus, when you are likely to do more covers than normal, allowing you to reduce your offerings, thereby making the preparation and service speedier. Another trend today, especially in high-end, chef-driven restaurants, is the menu degustation, or "tasting" menu: multiple courses are featured and paired with different wines, and offered at a set price that is much higher than an average dinner-menu price. You can adapt this to your own restaurant by offering a set three- or four-course meal that features some of your chef's signature dishes, accompanied by wine by the glass. Or do a dessert-sample plate, combining several smaller portions of your desserts on a large platter, encouraging your guests to indulge and experiment. The platter can also attract attention when it is being walked through the dining room, thereby acting as a merchandising tool.

# 2. *Menu Pricing*

You've attracted the "right" customers to your restaurant and have already impressed them with your ambiance, décor, and well-trained service employees. Now you must present them with a menu that will not only satisfy their tastes but also maximize your profit.

There are two methods for setting prices for your menu. The first is to note your competition's prices for similar items and price your own accordingly. The second method is to cost out each menu item and price it according to your desired food-cost percentage. For example, to achieve a 33 percent food cost, multiply the cost of the ingredients by three. This strategy will give you a rough starting point, and it may lead to the weighted-average approach, by which items with a higher raw food cost are priced at a higher food-cost percentage — otherwise, the selling price would be too high. For example, the portion cost for filet mignon may be too high to sell at a 33 percent food cost, so you will adjust it according to "what the market will bear" or what your competition is charging. However, less expensive food items can carry a higher markup, and therefore a much lower food cost. Pasta, for example, can sell at a much lower food costs percentage than can steak. Bear in mind, though, that you can't take a percentage to the bank! Profits from an item with a high food cost can actually be greater than those with a lower food cost percentage. Contribution margins — the diference between menu selling price and the cost of the menu ingredients — are where your focus should be.

Operators often use a combination of the two pricing methods, charging what the market will bear, but keeping in mind the projected food-cost percentages and profit margins. There is a greater discussion of food costing in chapter 13, "Cost Control."

As menu prices increase, so too does the level of service, and therefore the price/value relationship between quality and service must be in

*Your menu* **127**

balance. Customers will be willing to pay for attention and service as long as the food quality meets expectations, and vice versa. Your style of restaurant and level of service have to correlate with the quality and presentation of your food.

## 3. Menu Design and Development

The written menu is, of course, your primary merchandising tool. What follows are some of the "tricks of the trade" you can use when developing and designing your written menu.

- The top right-hand side of a two-page menu catches the customer's eye first. This means the items of which you are proudest and on which you make the most profit go top right. Locate your next most profitable items top left and bottom right, respectively.

- If your menu is formatted in only one column, bear in mind that the top item will attract the most attention. Again, place your most profitable dish at the top of the list (rather than placing the cheapest item there, as most restaurants do). The second item in the column is the next most favorable position. In a long column, the bottom line is also a favorable position.

**KEY POINT:** The format you choose for your written menu can have a profound effect on your sales. One of co-author Brian Cooper's clients once asked him how customer preferences in a highly popular chicken franchise could be changed toward more profitable pasta and pizza selection, which would result in higher profit margins. Brian merely tore the menu down the middle and placed the pizza items on the right-hand side of the menu instead of on the left-hand side. There was an immediate, 30 percent increase in pizza sales.

- Help the customer to envision the dish by describing the method of preparation in your menu copy. For example, you can describe a piece of fish as grilled, pan roasted, or seared. You can further describe that fish by stating where it came from and what will accompany it on the plate. You could describe it as "Pan-Seared Chilean Sea Bass, Summer Vegetables and Creamy Mashed Potatoes." If sauces accompany the dish, include them in the item's description. Any other significant feature of the product should also be included. If the vegetables are organically grown, or if the breed of animal signifies high value (such as "Black Angus" beef), that should be stated. Wonderful menus use words that make the customer want to use their senses, to taste, smell, and feel the food.

For example, savor these examples of descriptive menu copy:

*"Braised Organic Chicken with Black Olive and
Rosemary Bread Stuffing"*

*"Seared Maine Scallops with Sweet Pea and Garlic Mashed Potatoes"*

*"Copper River King Salmon Grilled with Fingerling Potatoes,
Asparagus, and Rhubarb-Ginger Chutney"*

*"Brick-Oven–Baked Flat Bread with Caramelized Eggplant and
Roasted Peppers"*

*"Crisp Meringues with Passion Fruit Custard and Exotic Fruits"*

Font selection and your cover color, design, and art work are very important in communicating your style. You may want to have your menu's "look" professionally developed to tie in with your restaurant concept and décor.

Customers can be heavily influenced by a picture of a particular item. However, ensure that you prepare the item exactly as it is pictured, as that picture is an implied contract. If you do not meet the customer's expectations, you leave yourself open to complaints and even lawsuits. It will be well worth the investment to have the pictures professionally done, as they should be properly lit and styled.

Use "dialogue boxes" or icons (such as a small chef's hat) to emphasize or set apart items you want to promote.

If key ingredients are highly seasonable and their cost varies widely over the year, do not laminate the menu. If you do laminate your menus, you will be less likely to raise the prices to accommodate higher costs, because that will mean throwing out these expensive menus. Instead you may keep them — and lose money. Today, it is quite acceptable and very practical to print your own menus using your computer and printer. Doing so allows for more menu changes and greater flexibility with price changes, so that you can take advantage of seasonal ingredients.

*Your menu* **129**

There is no such thing as a "loss leader." If you promote your restaurant by discounting a major selling feature, you will attract customers only for the time of the promotion. It is far better to be known for your quality and consistency. Nonetheless, you may want to offer a special discounted price to attract customers during off-peak hours.

You can effectively use a blackboard or whiteboard to list profitable specials or the total menu itself. Doing so suggests value or freshness to the customer. But remember that the item at the top of the blackboard is going to be your largest seller, so make sure it is your biggest profit maker. If you run out of a menu item, you can easily remove it during service. You can also expand your menu easily by adding chef's specials or daily specials. A word of caution: the person writing the menu must have very legible handwriting.

If your concept allows, inexpensive "throw away" newsletter menus, printed on newsprint, can be used effectively as advertising flyers. Customers can be encouraged to take these home.

Regular specials work well. Co-author Brian Cooper once knew a restaurateur who featured a wonderful meatloaf on his Wednesday luncheon menu. Customers flocked to his door every Wednesday. However, when he moved it to his regular daily menu, it was a flop. Many pubs feature items such as "hot wings" on specific slow nights of the week. Such specials do not break the "no loss leader" rule, since they are acting as a lure to expand beer or beverage sales on these traditionally slow nights.

You would be wise to increase your average check through the sales of wine, bottled water, appetizers, and highly profitable desserts to customers in your restaurant. Since they are already in the restaurant, you might as well increase the amount of money they spend with you. Make the most of it while they are near and dear. Bottled-water companies will send a representative in to train your staff in successfully selling and promoting their product. Well-trained service staff who are adept at strategic "upselling" can work wonders. A word of warning though: upselling must be done with care. Any hint of a hard sell might put the customer off.

Customize the size of your menu to the amount of time you expect your customers to remain in your restaurant. A complicated large menu in a fast-turnover operation will keep customers from making a decision quickly. They will be in the restaurant longer, thereby affecting the number of covers you will be able to sell to in a busy day. Very large

**130**   *Start and run a restaurant business*

menus are usually not a good idea in any case. Aside from creating the necessity for larger inventories, they imply to many the "out of the freezer, into the deep fryer, onto the plate" syndrome synonymous with tasteless, "rubber" food. Keep your menu simple, with enough items to address the normal variety of tastes in your market segment but not so many that you cannot be proud of, and even passionate about, the items you do offer.

You should consider removing from your menu any item that sells less than 10 percent of the total covers in your restaurant. If the item is a highly profitable one, you may want to try to turn it around by repositioning it on the menu, renaming the dish, or writing more interesting copy. Continue to track its popularity after you have made the merchandising changes. If it still doesn't perform, take it off the menu.

Leave room on the menu for seasonable items. It provides an opportunity for your kitchen brigade to introduce new, profitable dishes during seasons when product availability is high. You can remove these when such bargains are no longer available. Many restaurants revise their menus seasonally or at least in the spring and fall.

Ensure that not everything is prepared using the same piece of equipment (grill, fryer, sauté, etc.) Having everything grilled or fried will slow down your service and often result in staff falling over each other. Design your menu so that items can be prepared at different stations using various pieces of equipment.

When developing the menu, take into account the skill level and expertise of your staff. You can always consider purchasing some items from outside sources to supplement those made in house by your staff. Small restaurants may not be in a position to have a pastry chef, but excellent pastry items can be purchased and easily plated, adding a sauce and fresh fruit garnish to make them look as if they had been made on the premises.

Your china, plates, bowls, and flatware must all work together with your menu. The size and shape of your plates will affect the presentation of your food.

## 4. Developing a Wine List

Developing a wine list that is exciting, complements your menu, and is profitable is no small task. Wine is meant to go with food. Each bite should be enhanced by each sip, and vice versa. You and your chef should sit down and discuss your wine list at the same time as you develop your menu. Simply filling up a wine list with popular brands at affordable prices is not enough. Consider the following ideas when deciding which wines to feature with your menu:

- ☞ Balance is the key. Try to match the wine to the primary taste in the dish. For example, a heavy meat dish containing lots of fat and oils should be matched with a red wine having strong tannins (the astringent taste that comes from the grape skins). These elements will cut through the fatty, oily residue of a lamb or beef dish and refresh the pallet for the next bite. Similarly, a light, crisp white wine will enhance the subtle flavor of a fish dish. Clichéd as it may seem, creating this balance usually means white wines and rosés with seafood and light meats, and red wines with heavier, fattier red meats. This is not to say you cannot be a little adventurous — a Gewürztraminer with a spicy Mexican dish, for example — but always keep the tastes of your primary market in mind! If you have an extensive dessert-wine list, be certain your desserts themselves are not sweeter than the wines with which you pair them.

- ☞ If you specialize in a traditional regional cuisine (e.g., Northern Italian), you will have a better chance of achieving the perfect match of food and wine if you offer wines of the kind that have been matched with that cuisine over centuries.

- ☞ If your market is relatively traditional, offer choices of the traditional Old World (European) wines with similar — but often less expensive — New World wines from Australia, South Africa, Chile, and Argentina, to name but a few excellent wine-producing countries. Don't forget North American wines, either. Both the United States (most notably California, the Pacific North West, and New York) and Canada (Ontario ice wine!) have great reputations.

- ☞ Pay attention to your own area. Find out which are the best-selling wines in your region and, at a reasonable markup, carry a few favorites that match your menu.

- ☞ Don't forget the house wine. A choice of domestic and imported house wines by the glass and the carafe might end up being your best-sellers and providing you with the best profit margin.

**132**   *Start and run a restaurant business*

☞ Offer a flight of wine with a set menu. Doing so will allow customers to experience several wines without the pressure to choose just one!

☞ Finally, you must consider availability. There is no point selecting wonderful, exotic, and obscure wines to go with your food that then become very popular with your customers, only for you to discover you cannot obtain them anymore. Wines can have a limited supply, the wine agent may no longer represent that winery, or the vintner has stopped producing the wines you want. Many difficulties may arise. You can overcome some of these difficulties by finding a good wine agent or — better yet — agents. Shop around for someone who knows wine and the wine business, and is willing to sit down and get to know you and your menu.

## 4.1  Wine pricing

Wine sales can offer a huge boost to your bottom line. It is not uncommon for wine to carry a 300 percent markup. Your average bottle price should be in line with your food menu prices. You can carry a few expensive bottles on your wine list so that it makes your other bottles appear more reasonable!

Naturally your wine prices should reflect the level of service and pricing structure of your food menu. A $500 bottle of Chateaux Margaux is unlikely to be sold to a clientele who are planning to spend $50 to $60 for their meal. Remember, too, that the more expensive the cost of the wine, the less of a markup it will bear. A $10 bottle of wine might easily be sold for $25, but an $80 bottle of wine cannot be marked up to $200 and still be expected to sell, unless it is a unique and/or difficult to obtain vintage.

## 4.2  Designing your wine list

Your wine list, like your food menu, should be pleasing to the eye and easy to read. Bear in mind that if many of your customers are aging baby boomers, they are, perhaps, more and more interested in wine but less and less able to read fine print!

If you wish to list your wines in the traditional manner, place your white table wines first, follow them with reds and then sparkling wines, and place your dessert and fortified wines last. Beers, cocktails, spirits, and after-dinner drinks such as ports, brandies, and liqueurs (cordials) can be listed on separate pages. Other common styles of presentation are by country and/or region of origin, by grape variety, or even by reference to the food-menu items the wine is intended to match.

If you are serving vintage wines in a fine-dining environment, however, you should include at least the following information for each wine:

- the full name of the wine
- the producer/shipper of the wine
- the country and region (if applicable) of origin
- the bottle size and vintage (if applicable)
- the price

**KEY POINT:** Include a taste description of the wine on your wine list, and offer any information about the region or method of production or aging that will ultimately be a selling tool.

Information that will appear on the wine bottles themselves may include the following terms:

*American Viticultural Area (AVA):* A delimited, geographical grape-growing area that has officially been given appellation status by the Bureau of Alcohol, Tobacco, and Firearms. Two examples are Napa Valley and Sonoma Valley.

*Appellation d'Origine Contrôlée (AOC):* The French system of appellations, begun in the 1930s and considered the wine world's prototype. To carry an appellation in this system, a wine must follow rules describing the area in which the grapes are grown, the varieties used, the ripeness, the alcoholic strength, the vineyard yields, and the methods used in growing the grapes and making the wine.

*Appellation:* Defines the area in which a wine's grapes were grown, such as Bordeaux, Gevrey-Chambertin, Alexander Valley, or Russian River Valley. Regulations vary widely from country to country. For example, in order to use an appellation on a California wine label, 85 percent of the grapes used to make the wine must be grown in the specified district. (See also *Appellation d'Origine Contrôlée.*)

*Bottled by:* Means the wine could have been purchased ready-made and simply bottled by the brand owner, or made under contract by another winery. When the label reads "produced and bottled by" or "made and bottled by" it means the winery produced the wine from start to finish.

*Estate-Bottled:* A term once used by producers for those wines made from vineyards that they owned and which were contiguous to the winery estate. Today it indicates the winery either owns the vineyard or has a long-term lease to purchase the grapes.

*Made and Bottled by:* Indicates only that the winery crushed, fermented, and bottled a minimum of 10 percent of the wine in the bottle. Very misleading.

*Meritage:* An invented term, used by California wineries for Bordeaux-style red and white blended wines. Combines "merit" with "heritage." The term arose out of the need to name wines that didn't meet minimal labeling requirements for varietals (i.e., 75 percent of the named grape variety). For reds, the grapes allowed are cabernet sauvignon, merlot, cabernet franc, petite verdot, and malbec; for whites, sauvignon blanc and sémillon. Joseph Phelps Insignia and Flora Springs Trilogy are examples of wines whose blends vary each year, with no one grape dominating.

*Negociant (Negociant-Eleveur):* A type of French wine merchant, mostly found in Burgundy, who buys grapes and vinifies them, or buys wines and combines them, bottles the result under his own label, and ships it. Two well known examples are Joseph Drouhin and Louis Jadot.

*Nonvintage:* Blended from more than one vintage. This allows the vintner to keep a house style from year to year. Many champagnes and sparkling wines are nonvintage. Also, sherry and the nonvintage ports, the tawnies and the rubies.

*Private Reserve:* This description, along with Reserve, once stood for the best wines a winery produced, but as this term lacks a legal definition, many wineries use it or a spin-off for rather ordinary wines. Depending upon the producer, it may still signify excellent quality.

*Produced and Bottled by:* Indicates that the winery crushed, fermented, and bottled at least 75 percent of the wine in the bottle.

*Vintage Date:* Indicates the year that a wine was made. In order to carry a vintage date in the United States, for instance, a wine must come from grapes that are at least 95 percent from the stated calendar year. (See also *Nonvintage.*)

*Vintners' Quality Alliance (VQA):* Canadian appellation designation. Seven premier wine-growing regions in two provinces have been designated. In Ontario, these are the Niagara, Lake Erie-North Shore, and Pelee Island regions; in British Columbia, the Fraser, Okanagan, and Similkameen Valleys, and the southern tip of Vancouver Island.

## 4.3  *Resource guide*

Below are listed some Web sites and books you may find helpful to consult when putting together your wine list.

www.foodandwine.com

www.winespectator.com

www.tastetour.com

www.restaurantwine.com

Foulkes, Christopher, ed. *Larousse Pocket Encyclopedia of Wine.* Paris: Larousse, 1996.

Johnson, Hugh, and Jancis Robinson. *The World Atlas of Wine.* New York: Mitchell Beazley, 2001.

Robinson, Jancis. *Jancis Robinson's Guide to Wine Grapes.* New York: Oxford University Press, 1996.

Walton, Stuart. *The Complete Guide to Wines and Wine Drinking.* London: Southwater, 2004.

# Chapter 11
# THE ART OF SERVICE

It has always amazed us that so many restaurateurs, after spending a fortune to design and build the restaurant of their dreams and hiring the finest chefs to develop a menu that expresses their dream, will then hire inadequate servers.

All your careful planning and preparation will be wasted if your service staff are incapable of expressing your dream to your customers. Your service staff are among the most highly rewarded employees on your payroll. They are commissioned salespersons who earn from 10 percent to 20 percent of the customer's check. Select and train them with care.

## 1. *Keeping Customers Satisfied*

As we have discussed, service is all a matter of attitude. A customer will be less irritated and perhaps more willing to forgive and forget the mistakes of inexperience as long as the server demonstrates that he or she is trying to be attentive and helpful throughout the dining experience.

According to the National Restaurant Association, customers ranked poor service as their number one complaint. Poor service is also the reason why most customers fail to return to a restaurant. Consider the following guidelines to good service, which can apply to all restaurants:

- Restaurants are service oriented and customer driven; servers should accept this as a challenge to provide excellent service.

- Servers should listen carefully to guests' requests and respond with a smile, not with a negative attitude.

- Never offer an excuse for poor service or ill-prepared food. Just apologize and fix the problem.

- All complaints should be addressed as quickly as possible and settled suitably, which may mean a "complimentary" meal, bottle of wine, cocktail, or dessert, depending on the severity of the complaint.

- Keep conversation regarding complaints simple and to a minimum. Phrases such as "I apologize," or "Thank you for making us aware," or "We appreciate your telling us" are all excellent ways to communicate your understanding of the complaint.

- Have your servers work as a team rather than solo. Nothing is more irritating to a customer than being told by a server that a request can't be taken because "I'm not your server."

## 2. *Service Styles*

There are several traditional service styles found in restaurants. The most formal and demanding type of service is known as French service and calls for the server to artistically prepare or cook the food in front of the customer. The chef provides the server with the chosen menu item portion-sized to prepare tableside. Using a portable stove (called a *rechaud*), the server cooks the meal in front of the customer, exactly to the customer's specifications, with as much flair as possible. A Steak Diane or a Caesar Salad prepared tableside by a well-trained waitperson can yield high prices. This style of service, for the most part, is a thing of the past in North America for several reasons. French service is very labor intensive, and a much higher skill level is required in the service staff. Servers must be better trained, better paid, and are usually harder to find. French service requires cooking over a *rechaud* on a moveable cart (called a *geridon*), so the seating in the restaurant must leave enough room for the *geridon* to be able to approach each table easily. This takes up premium seating space. In modern urban North American

**138** *Start and run a restaurant business*

restaurants, rents are often high, and giving up valuable seats can be justified only if the check averages can be increased accordingly. This is rarely the case. The most common remnant of traditional French service still in evidence in North America is the dessert trolley that some restaurants use to display desserts and pastries to each customer for his or her personal selection.

Many people today confuse French service with what is really Russian service, or platter service, as it is sometimes called. In Russian service, the food is completely prepared in the kitchen and then brought into the dining room on large, usually silver platters — thus the other commonly used name, "silver service." The wait staff then serves individual portions to each guest according to his or her individual taste and appetite. Banquet service is a variation on Russian service. Buffets are a more modern, self-serve variation of Russian service as well.

At the other end of the spectrum from French service is American plate service, in which everything is plated in the kitchen by the cooks and brought to the table fully prepared and exactly fitting the plate. This is the style that is most commonly used in North America today. Of primary importance in this service style is the correct placement of the plate in front of the guest. In the past, the plate was placed with the protein portion closest to the customer at the six-o'clock position on the plate, the starch portion at twelve o'clock, and the vegetable portion at three o'clock. The style of presentation has changed over the last decade, and food placement no longer always follows the old traditions. The predominance of American plate service in today's industry has lead to the growth of a wide variety of plating styles. Chefs go to great lengths to plate food attractively, and dessert plating in particular has reached the level of an art form. Chefs are using multiple sauces and ingredients on a plate to create variety in texture, color, and height. The trend has been toward oversized white plates to allow for maximum presentation area. It is important that your service staff be made aware of which part of the plate is the "front," so that it is presented to the guest in the way that the chef intended. This is especially important in a banquet service in which everyone is served the same dish.

For many years formal rules had wait staff serving from the customer's left and clearing from the right (except beverage service, which was served and cleared from the right). This is often not very practical with tables that are placed against the wall or against banquet seating, or built into booths. Today what is most important is for the wait staff to approach the table in the most unobtrusive way possible while still providing attentive service.

# 3. Front-of-the-House Considerations

Although the traditional service styles can enhance the dining experience, especially of a more traditional, fine-dining establishment, most critical is that the service be expedient, attentive, and allows the customers to feel relaxed and enjoy their meal and conversation with their companions. Good service should support, not intrude on, the customer's enjoyment of excellent food, drink, and good company.

There are a number of factors that an experienced server must evaluate as he or she waits on a table. A successful server should first determine the amount of time the customers have to complete their meal. Sometimes house policy can assume time requirements. Many restaurants with busy lunch rushes in urban business areas present the guest check with the coffee as a matter of convenience for lunch customers with pressing time limitations. Tactfully asking dinner customers if they are trying to make a show or after-dinner engagement will give the server the information he or she needs to know to make a decision as to whether or not to try to upsell appetizers or desserts or specialties that may take a little longer to prepare. Customers appreciate servers asking them their time availability as long as this time frame is followed precisely. An enjoyable dining experience can be ruined by having to ask over and over again for the check or by having to wait while the server runs the credit card through the point-of-sale cash register. This is not the sort of final, lasting impression of your restaurant you want your customers to take away with them.

To help your staff improve their service to your customers, try the following:

☞ Upselling is easy for good servers, and can be profitable. It will increase your profits as well as their tips. People are ready, often eager for suggestions on how they can increase their dining pleasure. However, be careful to do so with tact. Pleasant suggestions are fine, but any hint of pressure can tarnish the atmosphere of considerate, attentive service you and your wait staff have worked to establish.

☞ Encourage your wait staff to promote what your chef prepares best, especially the signature dishes — those for which you are known. However, your staff should be proud to serve every menu item. If a dish is not being well received or does not present well on any particular day, your staff should be encouraged to tell the manager and/or chef. Never allow your staff to make asides to the customers such as, "I wouldn't order the so-and-so today. It's just not up to par." If it's not "up to par," it should be taken off the menu. Your staff should never imply that anything on your menu is not of the best quality.

☞ Ensure that only the correct amount of familiarity is shown to your guests. This depends a little on your concept and the level of formality that your service intends. Friendly greetings may be acceptable, but never allow your staff to join in with conversations that are transpiring between your guests.

☞ Be certain your servers know your menu intimately. They must know all the ingredients in each dish (especially these days, when allergies seem more prevalent), and how each dish is prepared. They should also understand how your wine list complements your menu. Whenever you feature a new dish in your restaurant, gather the wait staff together with the cooks and discuss and sample it before service.

No doubt you have heard the saying, "The customer is always right." We agree that whenever possible, you should attempt to satisfy as many of the customer's needs as is reasonable. To gain a loyal clientele, you will often have to bend over backward and exceed customer expectations. Training and empowering your service staff is key in ensuring customer satisfaction when dealing with issues such as replacement meals, substitutions, or minor changes in menu items. The quicker your service staff can respond to a customer's request, the happier the customer will be. It takes only a minute for a server to return to a recently served table to check on the guests' satisfaction and, if need be, respond to any problem or request. But make sure that all problems or requests are followed up. For instance, nothing is more annoying than a server promising to return with more bread, then showing up with dessert menus at the end of the meal, having forgotten all about it!

# 4. Dealing with Difficult Customers

"Meet and exceed your customers' expectations," is an old but very valid service guideline, and nowhere is it more important than in dealing with customer complaints. If you can address a customer's difficulty up to and beyond his or her expectations, before that customer leaves your restaurant, the customer will remember your response much more than the original problem. You can turn a potential disaster into a triumph by responding to a complaint with an "above and beyond the call" attitude.

*The art of service* **141**

Staff, managers, and cashiers should be trained to elicit the confidences of your customers, if they seem dissatisfied, before they finish their meal or leave the restaurant.

Never argue with any customer about a complaint. Offer a brief explanation if there has been a miscommunication but do not make excuses. The customer does not want to, nor should they have to, hear them. Any difficulty with an order should result in the customer not being charged for that item. The liberal use of "comps" can go a long way to soothe a customer whose dining pleasure has been compromised by a service error. The appeased customer will probably be more impressed by your service than if they simply enjoyed an uneventful meal.

Occasionally, however, you will encounter an "impossible" customer who seems to make it his or her raison d'être to complain about the food, the service, even the décor whenever he or she dines out, often taking out a bad day at the office on your staff. The best thing that you can do in this case is accept their complaints gracefully, try to offer a modest substitution to their order, and offer to remove the offending menu item from their bill, to satisfy their complaint and preserve your good reputation.

**KEY POINT:** It is far easier to keep an existing customer contented and promoting your restaurant or pub than it is to cope with a dissatisfied customer who will tell all of his or her friends about your failings. Whenever possible, all complaints should be settled before the customer leaves your restaurant. However, once in a while, you will encounter a customer who will not be appeased by the offer of a treat or a discount, and who will speak the dreaded words, "I'm never going to come back." Co-author Brian Cooper dealt with this situation by striking an ingenious mutual agreement with his toughest competitor. Whenever a customer at Brian's restaurant was dissatisfied and refused all offers to make good, Brian would offer to provide a free meal to the unhappy guest at his competitor's restaurant. His competitor, likewise, would appease dissatisfied customers with an offer of a free meal at Brian's restaurant. It always worked! The guests always accepted the invitation. They always came back.

# Chapter 12
# MARKETING

Once you've created your restaurant, it's time to open the doors, fill the seats, and build up your business. We discussed the importance of developing a pre-opening marketing strategy in chapter 3, "The Business Plan: Feasibility Study." Creating excitement around the opening of the restaurant and focusing on marketing after opening is the next phase. This effort will be an ongoing challenge and will include several different approaches, including the use of advertising and marketing professionals.

Remember, the goal of your marketing strategy or plan is to help ensure that you meet your sales projections. Your strategies will focus on ways to increase the public's awareness of your operation, generate interest, and bring in your target clientele. The results of a successful marketing campaign will be more customers — and profit on your bottom line. We discussed the need to determine your demographics and customer profile in the first part of this book; now, this same information will be the focus of your marketing efforts. To make the most of your marketing budget, you must tailor your efforts to reach your target audience.

Since marketing will be an ongoing part of your business, your marketing strategy will change as your operation evolves. There is no magical formula for a successful campaign or promotion, nor is there a "right" amount to spend in relation to your projected sales. However, industry standards suggest that between one percent and three percent of your revenue be set aside for your marketing budget, and the questions of how and where to best to use those dollars are as important as how much to spend. You will want to investigate several media, including printed material, public relations, advertising in local publications and on the radio, and the Internet. Of these options, public relations and the Internet are the most cost-effective and can provide a fantastic return. The Internet is a growing medium and is an excellent tool. It's a great alternative to other obvious advertising options, such as television, where costs for air time and production are far too high for most independently owned restaurants. However, as we will explain later in this chapter, by means of a good public relations campaign, you can gain access to television air time as well as print (or "ink") in magazines and newspapers that would otherwise be unaffordable.

# 1. Ongoing Marketing Strategies

Marketing can be looked at as a large umbrella with several supporting spokes. Those supporting elements are advertising, sales, merchandising, public relations, and promotions, and they must all reflect, support, and communicate your concept. Understanding how these activities differ from each other is also important. What follows is a brief summary of each.

## 1.1 Advertising

One of the secrets of successful advertising is the careful selection of your source. Print, direct mail, signs and billboards, radio, and television all have advantages, but not all will be right for you. Investigate each before making your decision.

### 1.1a Print

Print media ranges from daily newspapers and community weeklies to tourism and special-event publications, and from food and travel magazines to play bills. Whatever your choice will be, print advertising can play an important role in your marketing campaign. You need to match the cost of the ad with the clientele you wish to reach, and keep in mind not only who will receive the ad, but also how many copies of the printed piece are being produced. Ad size is also important; your ads should never be smaller than business-card size.

**KEY POINT:** If you have a small initial marketing budget, get your business cards designed in a letterhead package by a professional graphic designer and use the card as your ad until you can afford larger ad space in newspapers and magazines or in the form of a brochure. Size doesn't always matter, but an ad or business card that is too small or has too many words on it is not advisable. Use a tag line or key message — "always fresh, always open," for example — and keep using it.

An important print tip: continue to advertise. Build up a reputation of advertising in a publication and keep it consistent. It is better to advertise every week than to do it randomly. Pick a day — for example, every Wednesday, if that's when your newspaper's food section is released — and place your ad there each and every week. Do it all year round instead of three times a week for only 20 weeks.

**KEY POINT:** Newspapers and magazines will often prepare simple ads for you if you have your own logo and you know what you want to say. Local radio stations will too. Always make sure you're looking at marketing alternatives that you can afford and which will help you meet your goals.

### 1.1*b* Direct mail

When we say direct mail, we mean more than just your restaurant's name and address printed on colored paper. If you have designed (or have had designed for you) art work, a logo, or an image for your restaurant, you can use these to create simple, well-designed flyers that can be tailored around an event or used as invitations. They can be hand delivered, inserted into a community newspaper, or — yes — mailed directly to your customers. If you choose the latter method of delivery, you must factor in postage, but if you're lucky enough to have a generous budget, why not consider having your own postcard made? Such postcards are multi-purpose (you can use them as a direct mailer, as thank-you cards to customers, or as invitations to events), and two-sided pre-printed postcards can be cost-effective. One restaurant that has successfully used postcards as advertising is the Gramercy Tavern in New York City. The Gramercy encourages guests to write to a friend on the Gramercy Tavern postcard while at the restaurant, and in return, the restaurant mails the cards. Great advertising for the cost of a stamp! Specialty print shops sometimes do postcard packages that also include some design work, and most diversified print shops will do one-, two-, or four-color print.

### 1.1c  *Signage/billboards*

Whether it's on highway signs or subway platforms, signage is a great advertising option and one that has a lasting effect. Consider alternatives such as signs on benches in your neighborhood, hand-painted murals created on the side of your building by local art students, and multi-purpose posters that double as bus/subway ads.

### 1.1d  *Radio*

Find out which radio stations are your customers' favorites. You can ask your guests which station they prefer, check the demographics surveys you've already done, or try checking with local stations' sales teams. Choose the one that's right for you. Many stations offer packages that include limited creative or production costs (writing and taping the commercial) and air time.

To measure the effectiveness of your radio advertising, ask your customers how they heard about your restaurant when you're taking reservations, or create a contest that will incorporate this information. Doing so will help you understand if radio, print, or another means of advertising is what works best for you.

Radio programs that feature food and restaurant reviews can be useful to you. Try to have your restaurant reviewed, or find out if the hosts of such programs would be willing to interview you.

### 1.1e Television

As we have already mentioned, television is usually too expensive a medium for the average restaurateur. If you're truly set on doing television, try your local cable station, but make sure they're going to represent you well. Production costs to create television commercials are often equal to or greater than air-time costs.

It's much better to be seen on television as part of a program than to buy commercial time yourself. Try focusing part of your public relations campaign (see section **1.4** later in this chapter) on this area and pick a popular show that has on-camera guests or that goes out on location.

## 1.2 Sales

The sales aspect of marketing focuses on the guest once he or she has already decided to eat at your restaurant. Your sales team is your front-of-house servers, and they can heavily influence what customers order and how much they spend. A good server has the ability to boost your revenue, funneling it directly to your bottom line. The server is rewarded and often motivated by the increased tips that result from building the average check. Some successful strategies for building average checks include selling bottled water, wine by the glass, appetizers, side dishes, and desserts. The time and effort that you spend supporting your front-of-house servers will be well worthwhile. You can do this by providing them with training, including them in menu tastings and wine pairings, and by having them attend trade shows or exhibits. Wine representatives will often provide additional sales training and support for your staff. Increasing your servers' product knowledge and sales savvy is key to your servers' sales success.

## 1.3 Merchandising

Merchandising is a tool you can use to boost existing and potential customers' awareness of specific products. Anything from photographs to attractive presentations of raw or finished product can be employed to increase sales of a particular dish. But be careful here: food displays have a way of deteriorating and can often have a negative, rather than positive, effect on sales. Plated or raw food should be presented only if you have a refrigerated display case, and only if you are sure you can be tasteful and mindful of the product's life.

*Marketing* **147**

Propping can also be fun and effective. Try displaying culinary tools and old copper pots and pans, or using beautiful baskets to hold the fresh fruits and vegetables involved in preparing your signature dishes. An attractive display of your wine bottles can have impact and is not as troublesome as using fresh food, but if you choose to use vintage wine, consider the temperature in your display location so deterioration doesn't become an issue; wine should be displayed in an area where the temperature is constant (i.e., no fluctuations between hot and cold). If you use quality olive oils or infused oils, or interesting vinegars, these can also be creatively propped. Another suggestion: decorate your entrance with framed copies of your local press coverage, chef's awards, and memorabilia. (Having your servers recite the specials to the customers and describe the preparation of these dishes can also help merchandise your menu.)

## 1.4 *Public relations*

A good public relations campaign is one of our favorite marketing strategies. With or without a professional, a public relations campaign can get you the kind of press coverage that most restaurateurs just can't afford to buy. And there's a bonus to it, too: Since your restaurant is being covered by objective staff writers, reporters, or food journalists, readers/listeners are more likely to believe the claims made than if they were made in conventional advertising.

Participating in community events can be an important aspect of owning a "neighborhood" business, and can go a long way to creating goodwill among the locals toward your restaurant. Such participation may entail contributing a tray of house specialties to a fundraising event, sponsoring a little-league team, or providing a dinner for two as a raffle prize. Doing so can be a means of advertising your operation as well as thanking your community for supporting you.

You may also participate with other businesses in joint promotional activities in your community. For example, in Montclair, New Jersey, there is an annual fundraising event for the local middle school, during which a first-run movie is shown. The restaurants of the community feature set menus that night and contribute a portion of their sales back to the school. Such promotional events are fun and may help to raise your profile in the community — and increase your customer base.

Whatever you choose to do, maximize your publicity potential. Make certain the media know about the event and particularly about your involvement in it. Master the art of writing effective press releases, and find out to whom you should send or fax them and what the deadlines are.

Be sure you tap into this means of marketing, even if only to kick off your opening by inviting the media and taking the time to write your own press release highlighting the owner, chef, philosophy, and any upcoming special events. If you don't have the time to develop contacts with your local media or food writers and journalists, take the time to find someone who will do it for you, and regard his or her fee as money well spent.

## 1.5 Promotions

Put your restaurant space to good use by having food-based or wine- or beverage-based events to capitalize on sales and generate interest in your operation. Pick events that focus on your philosophy. Partnering with your wine or beer representative will help defray the costs. For example, if your cuisine is fresh and simple classic French, then have a Beaujolais party. If you are promoting California wines, do a special tasting menu that pairs a different wine with each course. If you want to feature your beer selection, have a beer tasting and match menu items you'd like to sell to that audience as the evening's hors d'oeuvres, even if it's your BBQ wings and chili to launch football season. Whatever you choose to do, make sure that it appeals to your customers, that it's fun, and that the general public can attend. Closed-doors events may get your bottom line moving but they won't get you much "ink." Only public events get press coverage; if that's your agenda, keep this in mind.

Co-author Brian Floody ran a very successful promotion in some of his neighborhood bars: the annual "Beaujolais Nouveau Wine Tasting Evening." This promotion was started to piggyback on the new interest in wine generated by France's brilliant marketing campaign in the early 1980s promoting the Beaujolais Nouveau wines from the Rhone Valley. The promotions were simple and cost-effective. A wine-tasting party was advertised by in-house posters and by personal invitations sent to all regular customers. The promotion was timed to coincide with the media hype around the annual November release of Beaujolais Nouveau. Some Beaujolais Nouveau was purchased and sold to interested customers by the bottle, and some was given away as door prizes. But the main focus of the evening was the sampling. Several local wine distributors were invited to come and offer the customers free tasting samples of their red and white house wines. The customers tried the various wines and voted for the wines that they enjoyed most. The individual white and red wines that got the most votes became the bar's house wines for the following year! The distributors were pleased by the exposure their products received, and, of course, if their wine won, they would enjoy the profits from having their wine purchased exclusively as the house wine for one year. Naturally the customers enjoyed the free wine and felt that they had some direct input into the choice of house wine in "their" neighborhood bar. The bar was able to provide an enjoyable "free" party as a thank you to its regular customers for past patronage and as a great introduction to any new customers, all at a nominal cost. The bar also gained an excellent excuse to use the rest of the year with customers who preferred a different variety of house wine, always followed by a pleasant "Be sure you're there to vote at next year's party!" The annual wine-tasting evenings became the favorite annual promotion among regular customers and staff alike.

For more information on how to get publicity, see *Getting Publicity* by Tana Fletcher and Julia Rockler, another title in the Self-Counsel Business Series.

## 2. *Professionals, and What They Have to Offer*

Your choices for advertising and promoting your restaurant are numerous and may require the services of a freelance specialist in public relations, advertising, graphic design, and/or media. In large urban centers, hiring public relations firms, advertising agencies, or graphic design companies can be expensive; you will incur both monthly retainer fees and ongoing costs, plus the price of the advertising space, air time, and printing. This is usually out of reach for the small restaurateur, unless, of course, you have unlimited resources. An alternative is engaging the help of freelance professionals. This can be a great cost-saving measure, as freelancers have lower overhead as well as significantly lower operating costs, and they can pass these savings along to you. After all, working with professionals will let you get back to your primary task — running the restaurant!

Your marketing image must communicate and support your concept, and should have a professional look. If you've hired a professional to help you create an image, listen to his or her suggestions and utilize his or her expertise; after all, that is what you are paying for. Once the final copy has been created and you are satisfied with the design, the

**150**   *Start and run a restaurant business*

look, and what is being communicated, use it consistently so customers begin to associate this look, logo, or design with your restaurant. Reinforce your image and maximize your exposure by using your logo, color scheme, font selection, and overall design as much as possible in all forms of communication: business cards, letterhead, print ads, posters, flyers, your menu, matchbooks, and public relations messages. You may also want to combine a "tag line" — a catchy information phrase that communicates a key message about your operation — with your logo or art work. It may not seem vital, but by developing your image, creating a logo, selecting things like color and type styles or fonts, you can communicate the "feel" of your operation, just as clearly as will your style of cuisine.

> **KEY POINT:** If you're hiring professionals to assist you, ask to see their portfolios and to speak with other clients for whom they've worked. Make certain their abilities meet your needs. Don't forget to get quotes and compare these with your budget. Discover how you'll work together with your artist or public relations specialist to measure your success and effectiveness. We recommend asking for a three-month or six-month plan that will be easy to assess and may include an opening event, a special event such as a wine pairing or tasting, a media event, and a limited advertising campaign.

## 2.1 *Sourcing the pros*

It can't be said too often: If your strength isn't marketing, go to professionals who can help you. You can start with the *Yellow Pages.* Look under "Advertising Agencies," "Public Relations Agencies," "Graphic Design," "Multimedia," and "Hospitality Consultants." You can also source creative talent through national directories and registries such as *The Agency Red Book,* published by the National Register Publishing Company. Your local library will also have directories of public relations firms that you can use as sources. Talk to people you know and find out who is handling the other restaurant accounts in your area.

Meet with several professionals to determine who will be able to provide you with the expertise to communicate your thoughts, feelings, and ideas about your restaurant to the public. You may choose a graphic designer and a public relations freelancer, and then personally contact the printing companies you wish to work with and the media in which you want to place ads. Ask your freelancers to help you in those areas with which you are unfamiliar. Freelance marketing pros are often well connected and can recommend people whose work is reputable.

**KEY POINT:** Some restaurants exchange or do "contra" deals with their advertising sales people. Contra deals are, in fact, bartering: meals and beverages are exchanged for ad space. Some freelancers will consider this as well, but many agencies don't. Don't try hiring students in the advertising or PR fields unless you're also willing to hire a student maitre d'. Consider it on the same basis — would you want a student-in-training speaking directly to your customers?

Make a list of your media or journalist contacts, too. Call each personally every month or six weeks to update them on new things you're doing and to let them know about any special events you're planning. If you don't have a reason to call them, invite them to drop by for dinner or to try a new menu item. If nothing else, call just to check that they're still there. Media personnel move around as often as chefs do. Keeping in touch also builds the relationship. When you talk to the media, always remember they're looking for something on which to do a story. Make sure you know what you want to say, and never speak "off the record" about any changes. Say only what you're willing to be quoted as saying. Represent yourself well and don't waste their time. Journalists are badgered by everyone and their chef. Tell them something that's important to you and your business, explain why it's worth an article, and thank them for their time. Public relations pros call this "pitching a story." The best way to do it is to watch or listen to a show or to read a journalist's regular articles to gain an understanding of what they cover and the tone they take. Once you're certain you have this, use the knowledge to choose what you should communicate to them.

## 3. Building Your Marketing Base

Marketing requires an understanding of who your customers are, where they are coming from and why they are there, and what they want from your restaurant. Only when you have a good handle on the answers to these questions can you successfully communicate what it is you have to offer them. Smart restaurateurs build databases on their customers in an attempt to better understand their habits, likes, and dislikes. You can gather customer information through the following means:

- conducting customer surveys
- collecting business cards in a prize-draw format
- noting requests customers make of servers and hosts
- using a computerized reservations system
- tracking Web site hits and e-mail addresses

**KEY POINT:** Don't ever sell your database to anyone. You'll lose your customers' respect and business.

## 3.1 A *loyal customer is free advertising*

The better you know your customers, the better chance you have of providing them with the level of service and quality that they expect.

Your customers will always be changing, wanting new items, and expecting you to respond to their new demands. You may find that the customer base you initially attracted will evolve over time. Changes in your customer base should be the basis for any changes you make to your menu offerings, wine selection, décor, and service style.

For a restaurant, marketing must be continuous. You must understand your target market's needs not only in the beginning when you develop your concept, but also as your restaurant evolves — which is exactly what will happen. No business and certainly no restaurant can afford to stand still and rest on past laurels. Dining and entertainment styles change, and so must your operation. A classic example of this kind of change faced one of us not so long ago.

Brian Floody operated one neighborhood bar for over a dozen years. In the first few years, the bar was very popular with the young singles set. Large food portions were served at relatively low prices to attract their attention. The beverage alcohol sales made up 80 percent of the total sales and food only 20 percent, an instance in which selling food as a "loss leader" was an excellent marketing tactic. The food sales managed to cover costs, and the profit was made on the alcohol sales. However, over the next five or six years, the "singles bar" business began to slow down as the established customer base began to age into their thirties. They began get married, get mortgages, have kids, drink less, and spend less time in the bar. They still patronized the bar, but they began to come in fewer times a week and when they did come, more often than not they came with their families to eat rather than to drink at the bar.

The problem that developed was that this age group was still the primary market. Younger drinkers were difficult to attract as they did not want to mix with the established 'older' clientele and they tended to go to other, more recently opened, "trendier" competition. Since new "singles" customers could not be attracted to replace the old customer base, the bar slowly had to become more of a restaurant in order to meet the changing needs of the original clientele. In order to maintain the same profit margins, the primary profit, now had to be made from the food sales, which had crept up to over 50 percent of the total sales. A careful juggling act was needed to make the food menu more profitable without upsetting the clientele. Food promotional nights took the place of an overall inexpensive menu. Less profitable items were 'buried' in inconspicuous parts of the menu and the more profitable menu items were vigorously promoted. To survive, the neighborhood bar had to become the neighborhood restaurant.

Remaining aware of the changing tastes of your customers is just as important as understanding their tastes in the very beginning, when you are developing your original concept.

## 3.2 *The role of service in marketing*

The National Restaurant Association states that there are three main reasons people eat out:

- ☞ No one has to cook or clean up.
- ☞ It allows for a change of pace.
- ☞ It's a treat.

Your challenge is to make people aware of your restaurant and to have them select it, but these things won't simply happen when you open the doors. They require planning — and a bit of luck. Often, word of mouth is the best mode of promotion. If you can make every customer want to tell their friends about your restaurant — their "new find" — you've succeeded.

Creating that wonderful experience that people will talk about requires good food, attentive service, and good value. Loyal customers are walking, talking, free advertisements for your business, so you may want to reward them and show your appreciation for their continued support. There are a number of ways you can do this:

☞ Greet them by name (if known) and show them to their favorite table. This initial contact with your guests is very important. You should make every effort to make your guests feel welcome, no matter how busy you are.

☞ Use a computerized reservations system that allows you to access information about their preferences when they call. Such a system can jog your memory about facts such as a customer's birthday, or wife's or husband's name. Keep staff aware of any changes in your guests' profile — food allergies, dietary restrictions, wine preferences — but make certain you staff understands that this information is confidential. These facts can help you and your staff treat your guests in a manner your guests will appreciate and for which they'll return.

☞ Make your guests feel important, especially when they are entertaining others at your restaurant, by providing prompt, efficient, outstanding service.

☞ Provide a complimentary, special hors d'ouevre (amuse bouche) or dessert from the chef. This gesture adds that special touch to the evening.

☞ Ensure that your guests have an exceptional experience so that they will want to tell their friends about it.

# 4. *Increasing Sales by Using the Five "Ps" of Marketing*

To gauge the success of your marketing plan, look at your budgeted or projected sales volume and compare it to the revenue that was actually

*Marketing* **155**

generated. You will want to look at ways to increase your sales volume without increasing your expenses. Consider the five "Ps" of marketing:

- product
- place
- people
- price
- promotions

## 4.1 *Product*

Look at your restaurant as the "product" you are selling. You are selling the total experience: food, beverages, and entertainment. Look at the entire package, then decide if there are ways that you can increase the sales. For instance:

- Consider your hours of operation. Can they be extended or altered to bring in more revenue? Are you closed on Sunday, yet in an area where Sunday shopping could drive business? Do you close too early to catch a potential after-theater crowd?

- Consider your menu. Does it need to be reworked or modified? If you're tracking sales, are there items that are not selling which should be replaced by potential high-sales dishes that have low food cost?

- Can you increase prices? Are there items on your menu that have not only perceived value but also lower food cost, such as smoked salmon? Look at where you would like to be in terms of revenue and develop a plan to get there.

## 4.2 *Place*

Place is an extremely important factor in your marketing plan. Where are you located? Is your restaurant easy to find? How effective is your signage? Can your customers see your restaurant from the road in time to stop or make a turn? Are there ways that you can improve the visibility? Are you capitalizing on a unique location, a destination, or an obscure "factory" setting to lure customers to your destination? Do you have parking issues? If parking is a problem, how can you increase your existing number of parking spaces? Do you offer valet parking now or can you consider it? Is public transit an alternative?

**156**   *Start and run a restaurant business*

Chapter 6, "Choosing Your Restaurant's Location," stresses that the suitability of a site must be investigated prior to signing a lease. However, even after opening, you may have some flexibility on items such as signage, lighting, and (to a degree) parking spaces. Maximize these, and look for other ways you can improve your location.

### 4.3 People

Have you properly identified where and who your customers are? Do they match the profile you used to develop your initial marketing strategy? If not, are you using the right tools for advertising? Re-evaluate your customer base now that you have opened and decide if you are targeting the right market.

### 4.4 Price

Where are your prices in comparison to your competition? Can you create a competitive advantage? Is there room for increase while maintaining customers' value for their dollar?

Is there a way to increase the sales of items such as appetizers and desserts? Try breaking down your sales into different menu categories so you can evaluate which menu items your service staff can try to promote.

### 4.5 Promotions

Consult the Promotions section in this chapter (section **1.5**). These activities create a level of interest and excitement that keeps your customers returning. Your promotions can focus on increasing awareness of a particular menu item by featuring it in a print ad and offering a "Two for One" price for it on a particular night. Some restaurants have successfully used discount coupons as a way of promoting themselves or have gotten themselves featured in a discount coupon book distributed by the convention bureau in their city or town. In addition, having an "early-bird special" during off-hours may help to increase sales by capturing new customers who want to take advantage of the discounted menu prices.

## 5. The Restaurant Critic: Friend or Foe?

The expression "There is no such thing as a free lunch" may well apply to the free advertising one gets with the restaurant critic's review in the local paper. Many restaurants have been swamped the evening following a good review, and just as many others have seen their business deteriorate due to a bad review. Bad reviews can read like horror stories, written by critics who don't consider the damage they can do.

If you have *any* advance notice you're about to be reviewed, notify your staff. Reviewers often come by in the first three months after a restaurant opens. Many are straightforward and will call ahead to say they're doing a review and ask for some background on your operation. However, some don't, so always be prepared. And here's a tip: If a reviewer is on the premises, try to convince him or her to join you for lunch the next day to taste an amazing dish the chef is introducing, or to return for breakfast and interview the chef or meet the co-owner at the same time. Two chances to impress are always better than one. Many critics won't be persuaded, but you can always try!

Good reviewers visit more than once before they write about you. Ask about their training and what made them want to be a food writer. It's important to know where they're coming from and what their knowledge base is and to respond accordingly. Finally, let reviewers know you're new to owning a restaurant, where you're from, that your front-of-house team is newly trained and all local, that the dessert was created by your pastry chef who once worked at a famous hotel or restaurant, that the wine was estate purchased — anything that's unique about your restaurant that might win them over!

## 6. *Web Opportunities*

Restaurants have traditionally been slow to embrace technology. But by now the old "dupe" system for writing checks and kitchen orders has been replaced in most operations by integrated POS systems that have remote printers in the kitchen and at various kitchen stations — hot, cold, and dessert — where the food is prepared and picked up. These computer systems have given the restaurant operator much quicker access to vital operating statistics. The popularity of menu items can be easily reviewed, and each server's average check can be calculated and compared against your company standard and the other servers' performances.

The Internet likewise offers opportunities, and you can get its technology working for you. The Internet has become a mainstream marketing tool for most industries with a product to sell. Restaurants are catching on and are creating a presence for themselves on the Web. A Web site can help to stimulate new business for your restaurant, and can be used to communicate your concept to potential customers.

When you build your Web site, there are a number of things you should be sure to describe:

☞ *Location:* Prominently feature your restaurant's address, phone, fax, and give directions via major routes to your restaurant. You may want to include a map or link to the tourism site in your town or city. Consider a system for allowing customers to make reservations by e-mail.

☞ *Hours of operation:* List the meal periods you serve along with the hours and days of the week when they are served.

☞ *Menus:* Include a copy of your current menu; it will interest and intrigue potential customers. You might also allow customers to use this menu to place take-out orders. Feature special holiday menus here too.

☞ *Upcoming events and promotions:* Give the dates, times, and a bit of information about any special events or promotions. Pictures can be used very effectively here.

☞ *Press kit and promotional material:* Feature biographies and photos of key personnel. Doing so will interest your customers and make it easier for media to access this information.

☞ *Guest-book page:* Provide space for visitors to write comments and give you feedback.

☞ *Links:* Investigate linking your site to others that complement your business. It is important to have links to your town or city site, Chamber of Commerce site, business-development sites, industry-related sites, and trade-journal sites.

☞ *Rewards:* Include a coupon for a complimentary beverage, two-for-one special, or some other "freebie" to lure people to your restaurant.

☞ *Recipes or tips:* Have your chef provide a monthly special recipe or cooking tip.

Your site can start small and grow along with your business. You can often incorporate into your site print material that you have developed

*Marketing* **159**

for other purposes. As your site grows, you may be able to attract advertising and offset the cost of maintaining your site through banner ads. The companies that advertise will want to see that you have a significant number of "hits" or visits to your site and will need to see a connection between their customer base and yours. Beware: This is not simply a one-time exercise! Once you've launched your site, you must continually update it to keep it current and interesting to potential customers.

## Chapter 13
# COST CONTROL

Congratulations! You have defined your concept and are getting closer to opening your restaurant. You've prepared the first draft of your menu, designed your facility, and found the best location. You know who you want as a partner and you have presented your friendly financial institution with your business plan and pro forma income statement. You still want to proceed in building and operating your restaurant or pub. Now it's time to plan the standards for your operation and to consider methods for ensuring that you make the most profit on your operation.

One of the primary reasons for restaurants failing is that the owners or operators have not set up a cost control system and so have no way of knowing if anything is missing or if costs do not measure up to standards. By the time a problem becomes evident, it may too late to take corrective action, as the damage already done can be quite serious to the financial well-being of the operation. This chapter discusses several cost standards that can help you maximize profits and keep waste and pilferage to a minimum.

# 1. Keep Control Systems Simple

Upon graduation from university, co-author Brian Cooper was hired as a food and beverage controller for a large European hotel. It was his responsibility to prepare a daily food cost analysis for the hotel by noon the following day. Unfortunately, these were the days prior to computerized, integrated point-of-sale (POS) systems designed to help you track inventory and keep on top of prices.

Brian's job was tedious. To prepare the daily food cost, he manually costed all requisitions of food that had been issued and transferred to and from the various kitchens in the hotel. He would compare those numbers with monthly inventory cost, and was usually correct within one-half of one percent. But it took three staff members to accomplish the task! Hardly a cost-effective use of those managers' time.

Today, however, with computer software, reports can be generated daily to give you a breakdown of your sales revenue by menu item. But calculating your cost of food will still require a bit more effort than just pushing a button on your POS system. Try using the following formula to calculate your cost of food:

**Opening inventory** (a dollar value for food already purchased and on hand at the start of the period for which you are calculating food cost)

*plus*

**Purchases** (a tally of all invoices for the period for which you are calculating food cost)

*minus*

**Closing inventory** (a dollar value for the food that hasn't been used to generate the sales revenue for the period for which you are calculating food cost)

*plus* or *minus*

**Adjustments** (subtract any food sent to the bar, the cost of employee meals, and any complimentary meals; add the cost of liquor transferred from the bar to the kitchen for use in recipes)

*equals*

**Cost of food**

This method requires a great deal of work — taking inventory and costing that inventory — and, for a small operation, may take more time and trouble than an "accurate" food cost is worth. Instead, you may decide to assign a ballpark number to your inventories — opening and closing — and just use your purchases for the period to determine the cost of food.

Food-cost percentages are meaningless on their own, but they become useful to management when compared to targets. Once you have identified a difference between actual and budgeted costs, such as higher-than-projected food costs, you can begin to investigate *why* the figure is higher, and then, most important, take corrective action.

> **KEY POINT:** Be sure that your accounting software program is adjusted to use only the revenue from food sales — rather than food and alcoholic beverage sales combined — to calculate the food-cost percentage.

There are a number of reasons why your actual food costs may be higher than your projections. There are also methods you can use to remedy these problems:

- *Waste:* Have your chef check on waste. Waste can result from incorrect trimming of meat, fish, and poultry, or from improperly cooked food — every meal sent back to the kitchen by a dissatisfied customer means a replacement meal provided free of charge to the guest. To avoid waste, improve the skill level of your staff through rigorous training and monitor their performance.

- *Pilferage or theft:* Are your staff eating on the line? Do you have policies regarding eating in the kitchen? Are items going out the back door and into employees' cars? How does your staff come and go from the building? Who is receiving your incoming food supplies? Are shipment weights being checked to ensure you aren't being short shipped? Is all food picked up from the kitchen accounted for by means of a guest check? Before you open your restaurant, be certain you have adequate security measures in place to ensure against theft.

☞ *Spoilage:* Food costs can skyrocket if food is being thrown away with no sales to offset the purchase costs. Purchasing too much of an item leads to spoilage if the food sits in the refrigerator or is left out at room temperature. Avoid spoilage by never purchasing more of an item than you will need, and see to it that all food is properly stored. (See section **8.** for more on storage.)

☞ *Improper portion control:* Your bottom line will take a beating if your staff prepares and serves portions that are too large. For example, if portion size for filet mignon is set at five ounces, the kitchen staff must cut the filet according to those specifications. You may consider having your meat purveyor provide you with portion-cut steaks if this is a problem, but once again, careful training of your kitchen staff can help keep portion size under control. Have your chef develop standardized recipes and plate presentations for all menu items, and see that the standards are followed.

☞ *Increase in raw food prices:* Have the actual costs of food products risen significantly since you did your food-cost projections? If so, your cost of food will be correspondingly higher. You can remedy this by trying to locate new suppliers. Alternatively, you can reflect that increase in the selling prices on your menu, or decrease the portion size. Occasionally, you may have to take an item off your menu and substitute another in its place.

☞ *Poor forecasting:* Your inventory is highly perishable and the window for selling it is small. Overproduction will result in waste. Develop the ability to accurately forecast how much of each item you will sell. (See chapter 4, "The Business Plan: The Financial Plan," for information on how to forecast.)

Costing out your menu items is a valuable control process. First, though, you must develop standard recipes.

# 2. *Standard Recipes*

Standard recipes are recipes customized for your operation that detail precise instructions for the preparation and cooking of each dish on your menu. Create a standard recipe for every item on your menu, and inform each of your chefs to follow it exactly.

There are several important reasons to standardize your recipes:

☞ *Consistency:* Naturally, customers expect a menu item to look and taste the same each time they order it. If you have staff turnover, standard recipes will help ensure consistency during the changeover.

☞ *Cost:* To forecast food and beverage costs, you must know exactly how much each item costs to prepare. Standard recipes make this easy by stating exactly how much of each ingredient is to be used.

☞ *Purchasing:* To budget funds to purchase sufficient stock, you must know the exact amount and cost of the products required.

☞ *Pricing:* Pricing depends to a large degree on cost. You set a menu item's price according to the profit margin you intend to generate from that item; therefore you must know how much its ingredients will cost.

☞ *Training:* Training your production staff is much easier if the standard recipe is written down clearly and precisely and is available for reference while working.

You can use Sample 10, "Standard Recipe," to document your standard recipes. Place the name of the dish at the top of the page along with the yield (the number of portions or volume a recipe can be expected to create). Follow this with a list of all ingredients and required quantities, then detail the method of production, cooking instructions, and the equipment needed.

Cost each standard recipe once it has been created. Cost out each ingredient not only for the unit in which it is purchased, but also for the actual amount needed in the recipe itself. For example, a standard recipe form for an omelet would state the cost of the purchase unit — a case of eggs (16 dozen eggs) for, let's say, $18.00. The form would also show the cost of the three eggs needed in the specific recipe (3 eggs = 27 cents). Items such as meats may change in size during preparation due to butchering and shrinkage during roasting, and these changes should be calculated and shown on the form. The standard recipe form also indicates the individual portion size as well as the number of servings anticipated from the recipe. A photograph of the proper visual presentation of a menu item is often included on the form, which is useful in the kitchen for training and reference purposes.

*Cost control* **165**

## Sample 10
# STANDARD RECIPE

Include photograph of dish for presentation

**Name of your restaurant:** _____

**Name of dish:** _____  **Date:** _____

**Number of portions/yield:** _____  **Portion size:** _____

Ingredient:                                                                 Amount/quantity

1.
2.
3.
4.
5.
6.
7.
8.

Method of preparation (include equipment needed):

Steps:

1.
2.
3.
4.
5.

Directions for portioning and plating (specify serving plate to be used)

Food-cost percentages can be calculated for each menu item by costing out the recipe (see Sample 11, "Food Cost Form") for each menu item and dividing that item's cost by the menu selling price, and then multiplying by 100. For example, if the cost of the Chicken Française is $2.95 and the menu selling price is $11.00, the food cost is 26.8 percent. This figure becomes important only when it is compared with actual results.

Computer spreadsheets lend themselves very well to use as standard recipe forms. When you update the cost of ingredients, the spreadsheet automatically recalculates the cost and profit margin for each menu item. Sales-mix information (the popularity index — i.e., the breakdown of sales by item) can be introduced from the POS system to allow for the calculation of an overall food-cost percentage and profit margin. Some POS systems even have built-in spreadsheet capabilities.

## 3. *Standard Purchase Specifications*

As you and/or your chef develop your menu, you will also develop the standard purchase specifications for the ingredients needed to create each dish. The standard purchase specifications are the exact purchase requirements for each ingredient. For example, suppose you decide to put a Grilled Chicken Caesar Salad on your menu. You decide that you want to use a four-ounce, fresh, boneless, free-range chicken breast. These attributes become your purchase specifications for that item.

You can now approach your poultry suppliers using these specifications, and you can make valid comparisons between competing suppliers' prices. If you were to ask your suppliers simply for chicken breasts, you might find a large discrepancy in prices. One supplier might be quoting you a price for what you have in mind, but another might be quoting on three-ounce, frozen, bone-in, regular chicken breasts. Naturally, quote number two would be substantially cheaper, but you would receive a product inferior to the one you have decided your recipe requires. Purchase specifications are essential to ensure quality and facilitate price comparisons when shopping around.

## 4. *Supplier Selection*

How do you go about selecting a supplier? This decision depends on several factors — provided your location allows you the luxury of choice. If you are situated in a small community or a rural area, you

*Cost control* **167**

## Sample 11
## FOOD COST FORM

Name of your restaurant _____

Menu item: _____ Meal period: _____

Date: _____

Number of portions/yield: _____ Portion size: _____

Cost per portion: _____ Menu selling price: _____ Food cost %: _____

| Ingredients | Quantity | Cost<br>AP   Yield %   EP | Total cost |
|---|---|---|---|
| 1. | | | |
| 2. | | | |
| 3. | | | |
| 4. | | | |
| 5. | | | |
| 6. | | | |
| 7. | | | |

Note: Remember to add the cost of garnishes, and you may want to assign a cost for bread and butter served with the meal.

To calculate the **Cost per portion**: Total cost of all ingredients ÷ Number of portions

Food cost % = Cost per portion ÷ menu selling price x 100

may find you have far less freedom regarding from whom you buy than you would in a more urban location.

Having reliable sources for your raw ingredients directly affects your menu. There is no point in putting Fresh, Home-Made Guacamole on a menu if you cannot obtain quality avocados at reasonable prices year-round.

Many questions must be answered when selecting a supplier. A few of the most pressing ones are —

- ☞ Is the supplier able to provide you with exactly what your purchase specifications require? Can they do it year-round?
- ☞ Do they have the appropriate government licenses to operate as food wholesalers?
- ☞ Are their facilities sanitary? Paying them a visit, if possible, can be very revealing!
- ☞ Do they have appropriate cold storage? Do their delivery vehicles have the appropriate temperature controls?
- ☞ Are their prices competitive?
- ☞ Is their service reliable?
- ☞ Can they deliver to you at appropriate times of the week? Of the day (e.g., not during your lunch rush!)?
- ☞ Can they provide emergency delivery service when you run out of product unexpectedly?
- ☞ Is there a minimum order required?
- ☞ What kind of payment terms do they require?
- ☞ Do they have a proven track record? Check their references!

Finding a good supplier requires more than just opening the phone book. Often, word of mouth is the best source for information on suppliers. Can your friend the chef down the street, for example, recommend a good bakery? Does your local restaurant association have an approved supplier list? A little trial and error is usually unavoidable, and there are times when you will have to settle for less-than-ideal situations. Try to have more than one supplier for your various ingredients. If you keep your options open and shop around, you will keep your suppliers from taking your business for granted, and in the long run, you'll receive better prices and service.

*Cost control* **169**

# 5. Purchasing

Once you have established suppliers, you will need to create a purchasing system — a set of procedures, including documentation, to ensure that you consistently acquire the right ingredients at the right time and for the right prices.

First you must decide who will do your purchasing. If you are a chef/owner, you will probably want to do it yourself. If not, assign it to someone who is trustworthy and knowledgeable enough to do the job. In smaller operations, this person will often be the chef or the general manager; in larger operations, a specialist whose only job is purchasing. Whichever the case, take care in choosing a purchaser. After all, he or she is authorized to spend the company's money.

All purchasing should be done through the purchaser. Obviously, confusion will reign if every cook who runs short of a product is allowed to go to the phone and order more.

Like cash, purchases are controlled by a paper trail of documents that follow the "chain of custody" of the purchased assets. This trail runs from purchasing to receiving and storage, as the purchased goods are delivered, accepted, and put away. From storage, the goods are "issued" to the kitchen or bar, where they are prepared and sold to the waiting customers. *Every step of this journey must be documented.*

The initial documents are a purchase order (P.O.) and/or an order sheet. The purchaser should use a P.O. if purchasing nonperishable goods that are not in immediate demand. See Sample 12 for an example of a purchase order.

However, unlike many industries, most product purchased by a restaurant tends to be perishable and is needed quickly. Purchasing over the telephone, by fax, or online are the industry norms. There is no signed contract between the purchaser and the supplier, and therefore a certain amount of trust is essential — another reason to select your suppliers with care.

Purchasing over the telephone requires that you be certain the supplier is aware of the exact purchase specifications of the products you are ordering. The best way to do this is to send a list of the appropriate purchase specifications to the supplier at the outset of the relationship. When placing an order by telephone, the purchaser uses an order sheet, which, like a P.O., should contain the supplier's name, the date, the

**170**  *Start and run a restaurant business*

## *Sample 12*
## PURCHASE ORDER

From: Your Restaurant
1532 Food Street
YourTown, NY 00000
Phone: 555-0000
Fax: 555-0001

No. _____

Date _____

*Please include this purchase order number on all correspondence.*

To _____

_____

_____

Terms _____ Delivery Date _____

| QUANTITY | DESCRIPTION | PRICE | AMOUNT |
|----------|-------------|-------|--------|
|          |             |       |        |
|          |             |       |        |
|          |             |       |        |
|          |             |       |        |
|          |             |       |        |
|          |             |       |        |
|          |             |       |        |
|          |             |       |        |

TOTAL _____

Special Instructions _____

_____

_____

Authorized By _____ Date _____

171

items purchased, and the number and price agreed on for each. A copy of the order sheet should be sent to the receiver.

A purchaser should shop around among suppliers for the best price and payment terms. The purchaser must know the purchase specs intimately so he or she can select replacement products if the original purchase specs cannot be met. Purchasers must be able to take advantage of discounts offered by suppliers and know how much capital they can invest in a product, especially if purchasing a large quantity can result in a significant saving.

## 6. *Par Stocks*

Par stock is simply the amount of any given product you decide you want to keep on hand to last through a given period of time. Establishing par stocks will help you ensure that your restaurant has enough product to get through even the busiest period. Par stocks can also be used as the basis for completing an order sheet.

For example, a bar's par stock for bar-brand vodka for one day might be six bottles. Therefore, at the beginning of the day, the bartender must see to it that there are six bottles of bar vodka behind the bar. At the end of the day, or the next morning before opening, the bartender on duty does a mini-inventory of bar vodka. Let us suppose that there is only one bottle left. To bring the bar vodka back up to par, the bartender must requisition five bottles of bar vodka from the storeroom. The storeroom par stock would work the same way. If the bar manager has decided that there should be two cases (24 bottles) of bar vodka on hand in the storeroom after receiving the weekly liquor order, then if at the end of the week when the bar vodka is counted there are only five bottles left, 19 bottles must be ordered.

Par stocks can be established for virtually every type of product used. The par stock should be set by establishing how much of a product will be used up over the given time period at the highest sales volumes expected. Add 10 percent more as a safety margin. If, for example, on the busiest day of the busiest week the bar uses a little less than five bottles of vodka, then six bottles of vodka should do the bar through the busiest day and would be an appropriate daily par stock. If the liquor delivery comes once a week, and 21 or 22 bottles of vodka is the most you have used in your busiest week, a weekly par stock of 24 bottles should be sufficient.

**172**    *Start and run a restaurant business*

Resist the temptation to overstock your inventories to make certain you do not run out of product during busy periods. Capital invested in inventory is not making you any money and is costing you valuable storage space. Keep par stocks as close to the level of actual usage as you can. Make exceptions to this rule only if you can purchase a large amount of product at sufficiently discounted prices to make the money saved greater than the cost of storage and the interest your capital might otherwise have earned.

# 7. Receiving

Receiving must be done carefully. Goods left sitting unattended on a receiving dock or at the back door are in danger of being stolen or damaged. Delivery personnel have been known to take advantage of less-than-alert receivers by passing inferior or damaged goods or even "shorting" counts. The receiver's primary responsibilities are to secure delivered goods quickly and to check that the items delivered match the items ordered (as per the order sheet) in three ways: quantity, price, and quality.

The quantities of the goods delivered must be counted and compared to the quantities indicated on the order sheet *and* those on the delivery invoice (the supplier's document describing the goods sent, just as the P.O. or the order sheet describes the goods the purchaser ordered). These two documents should be in agreement. If they are not, the receiver and the delivery person must agree on the discrepancies, note these down, and sign or initial the invoice and the order sheet. Doing so ensures that the supplier will deduct from the bill the price of any goods that were not delivered or not accepted by the receiver. The receiver should not accept damaged or inferior goods and also must inform the chef if expected products are back ordered and will not be available for use when anticipated.

The receiver must also compare the prices on the order sheet to those on the invoice and, along with the delivery person, initial any differences — unless, of course, the purchaser has already agreed on prices with the supplier in a pre-negotiated contract. In such a case, the prices may not even be on the order sheet, and it is the purchaser who must follow up to make certain that the prices negotiated were indeed the ones charged.

The most difficult duty of the receiver is verifying the quality of the goods: the goods must match the purchase specs, their weights must be

Cost control **173**

correct, their temperatures must be appropriate (e.g., frozen products must be frozen), they must not be damaged, and their packaging must be intact.

Quantity, quality, and price should be meticulously checked. Once the receiver signs the invoice indicating that the order is accepted, it may be too late to remedy discrepancies between the order sheet and the goods delivered.

**KEY POINT:** If your operation is a small one, it may be impractical for you or your receiver to check every case. The cost of the time spent weighing every package and case and checking the temperatures of all refrigerated goods would outweigh the benefit of the control procedure. This "cost/benefit ratio" must always be taken into account when initiating any kind of control procedure. If you cannot afford the time to do thorough checking of a large order, make careful random checks of the less expensive items, but take care with the expensive goods, such as meat and seafood.

## 8. *Storage*

There are three main rules regarding food storage:

1. Have a place for everything, and everything in its place
2. FIFO (First in, first out)
3. Keep it locked up

As soon as possible following deliveries, move all goods to the appropriate storage areas. Create storeroom or refrigerator shelf space before a shipment of goods arrives, rather than waiting until the goods are sitting on the loading dock. As mentioned above, delivered goods left on loading docks or at back doors are naturally at a higher risk of theft. In addition, refrigerated and frozen products deteriorate quickly if not placed in proper cold storage.

The first rule, "Have a place for everything, and everything in its place," means exactly what it says. Organize your storage areas into well-marked sections and store items only in the correct section. Not only will the item be easy to locate, but this practice can also help prevent waste — for example, of milk, which is over-ordered because a portion of the last dairy delivery was stored in the fresh produce section of the walk-in refrigerator and was therefore overlooked.

Group items together by kind. All the products that usually come from one supplier should be in the same general area of the storeroom. Dairy products, meat, poultry, and fresh produce should all have their own areas in the walk-in refrigerator. To save yourself and your staff time, store your most often-used ingredients nearest the door.

The careful storing of products in their correct places will also make it easier for you to take a quick and accurate physical inventory. Inventory sheets, such as the one in Sample 13, created to record a physical inventory, should list the items in their geographical order in the storeroom (or walk-in refrigerator) so the inventory taker need only walk by, counting items in the order in which they are encountered.

FIFO, meaning "first in, first out," is an old and important adage in the restaurant business. To minimize spoilage, rotate your stock, especially your perishables, so that the oldest items (first in) are used up (first out) before newer stock. In practice, this involves moving any existing inventory aside and placing newly delivered items behind it.

Another simple adage to keep in mind regarding storage practices is "Store cooked above raw." This statement refers to the safe practice of storing already prepared products on shelving above raw, uncooked products in a walk-in refrigerator. It should be general practice to cover all stored products.

All inventory should be kept under lock and key. This is a vital precation, and in some jurisdictions is legally required with regards to beverage alcohol. A simple padlock will deter most employee pilferage and impulse theft. In practice, it might be inconvenient to keep a walk-in refrigerator locked in a working kitchen with cooks coming and going, but the lock should go on as soon as access is no longer required.

# 9. *Perpetual Inventories*

Perpetual inventories are systems that document the movement of product in and out of a storage area. A manager, receiver, or storeroom

Cost control **175**

## Sample 13
## INVENTORY

LOCATION _____ PRICED BY _____ DATE _____
(Kitchen, Storeroom, Wine Cellar)
CALLED BY _____ DATE EXTENDED BY _____ DATE _____
ENTERED BY _____ DATE EXAMINED BY _____ DATE _____

|    | Quantity | Unit | Description | ✓ | Unit Price | Extension | Total | ✓ |
|----|----------|------|-------------|---|------------|-----------|-------|---|
| 1  |          |      |             |   |            |           |       |   |
| 2  |          |      |             |   |            |           |       |   |
| 3  |          |      |             |   |            |           |       |   |
| 4  |          |      |             |   |            |           |       |   |
| 5  |          |      |             |   |            |           |       |   |
| 6  |          |      |             |   |            |           |       |   |
| 7  |          |      |             |   |            |           |       |   |
| 8  |          |      |             |   |            |           |       |   |
| 9  |          |      |             |   |            |           |       |   |
| 10 |          |      |             |   |            |           |       |   |
| 11 |          |      |             |   |            |           |       |   |
| 12 |          |      |             |   |            |           |       |   |
| 13 |          |      |             |   |            |           |       |   |
| 14 |          |      |             |   |            |           |       |   |
| 15 |          |      |             |   |            |           |       |   |
| 16 |          |      |             |   |            |           |       |   |
| 17 |          |      |             |   |            |           |       |   |
| 18 |          |      |             |   |            |           |       |   |
| 19 |          |      |             |   |            |           |       |   |
| 20 |          |      |             |   |            |           |       |   |

**Total** _____

clerk uses a sheet to note when and how many of which items are put into or taken out of a given storage area. Perpetual inventory sheets, such as Sample 14, can be formatted for daily or weekly use, and are kept inside the locked storage area. Sometimes individual inventory cards, called bin cards, are used for each and every item kept in the storeroom. If properly kept up to date, these systems can form a detailed paper trail of the movement of the restaurant's purchased assets, from receiving to service, and can help pinpoint any loss of product.

Perpetual inventory systems can be very successfully computerized and integrated with cash systems in large retail operations in which individual items are sold in much the same condition as they were purchased. In our experience, however, these systems are less effective in dealing with food that is purchased in the form of many individual ingredients that are then sold together as a meal. Nonetheless, as integrated, computerized POS systems become more sophisticated, they may become as excellent a tool for inventory control as they already are for recording and classifying sales.

# 10. *Issuing*

Issuing procedures control the movement of goods within your operation. Your paper trail continues at this point with the use of requisition forms — forms that a kitchen or bar uses to order products from storage, and to record the movement of any product from storage up to the kitchen or bar, or between the kitchen and bar.

For example, if a bartender needs five bottles of bar vodka, he or she would fill out a requisition. (Requisition forms are sequentially numbered and are usually in duplicate or triplicate.) The bartender indicates the products needed, and dates and signs the form. He or she gives one copy to a manager and keeps one copy to attach to the bar cash-out sheet. (Sometimes a third copy is sent to the bookkeeper.) The manager then proceeds to the liquor storeroom and "fills" the requisition by taking out five bottles of bar vodka and delivering them to the bartender, who then checks them off on his or her copy of the requisition form. The manager normally adjusts the perpetual inventory sheet in the liquor storeroom to show that five bottles of bar vodka have been taken, and initials his or her copy of the requisition form and leaves it with the perpetual inventory sheet in the locked storeroom. In order to steal anything, a bartender and a manager would have to work together and

*Cost control* **177**

## Sample 14
## PERPETUAL INVENTORY/BIN CARD

Item _____  Item No. _____

Location _____  Max. Quantity _____  Min. Quantity _____

**ORDERED OUT**

| Date | Order No. | Quantity | Date Due | Date | Order No. | Quantity | Balance |
|------|-----------|----------|----------|------|-----------|----------|---------|
|      |           |          |          |      |           |          |         |
|      |           |          |          |      |           |          |         |
|      |           |          |          |      |           |          |         |
|      |           |          |          |      |           |          |         |
|      |           |          |          |      |           |          |         |
|      |           |          |          |      |           |          |         |
|      |           |          |          |      |           |          |         |
|      |           |          |          |      |           |          |         |
|      |           |          |          |      |           |          |         |

**IN**

| Date | Order No. | Quantity |
|------|-----------|----------|
|      |           |          |
|      |           |          |
|      |           |          |
|      |           |          |
|      |           |          |
|      |           |          |
|      |           |          |
|      |           |          |
|      |           |          |

alter both copies of the requisition form. And even if they did so, either the bar par stock or the storeroom par stock will not balance, and they would run the risk of discovery.

Your paper trail, which started with the purchaser's order sheet, has to this point tracked the product from the initial order through receiving to storage and finally to the bar or kitchen. Here the POS system takes over in documenting the movement of the product from server to customer.

# 11. *Service Area Control*

The movement of product from your kitchen (or bar) to your servers and ultimately to your customers presents special challenges. Food can be stolen directly by the kitchen staff, spoiled or burned in the cooking process, spilled, dropped, or stolen by a server. The server can order the wrong item, deliver a wrong item, or leave food waiting until it is cold. Many, many problems can occur to prevent you from maximizing the profit on the product you have purchased and for which, up to now, you have so diligently accounted. At this stage especially, management eyes must be kept wide open, and control systems — ordering, pick-up, and POS procedures — must be adhered to rigorously.

The heart of the front of the house in terms of control is the cash register or POS system. A good cash register is invaluable. Of course, in a small, mom-and-pop operation, ordering through the old-fashioned handwritten, guest-check system can still work fine. But the larger and busier you become, the harder it is to keep track of sales and product. If you plan on staffing your restaurant with anyone beyond your immediate family and trusted friends, you must invest in a good cash system. The simplest cash system will record your sales and compile sales totals by type of sale (food, wine, beer) as well as by server. It will provide various tax totals to simplify your tax remissions. And it can often provide popularity indexes, which tell you how well your various menu items sell in relation to one another. All of this will be important information when you order and budget and can be very useful when you redesign your menu for the next season.

However, the cash register's primary purpose is to keep a record of all product sold and to ensure that the appropriate amount of money was received in return. The importance of having all outgoing product "rung in" to the POS system cannot be overemphasized.

*Cost control* **179**

**KEY POINT:** The following brief summary of an old restaurant tale demonstrates the value of the cash register perfectly.

A restaurateur was concerned about the profitability of a restaurant he owned in another city. The restaurant never seemed to be able to convert the high sales he witnessed when he was in town into a large net income. He hired a prestigious and expensive security agency to send in professional "spotters" to watch his staff work. After more than a month, the head of the security agency came to him and, rather chagrined, explained that they could find no fault with the way the employees worked. They were efficient, reliable, and friendly, and indeed seemed to be doing a great job. "Were all the sales being properly recorded in the cash register?" the owner asked. The security specialist said his spotters were especially careful to note that all sales were always rung in, whether at the main cash register in the restaurant proper or at the second cash register in the holding bar area. Whereupon the restaurant owner responded, "What second cash register?"

The restaurant staff and managers had put up their own cash register to defray any spotters' suspicions of theft and were simply keeping all the revenue rung into that cash register and destroying the sales tapes. The cash register was carefully hidden away whenever the owner or the accountant was coming into the restaurant.

Of course, random security spotting from the very beginning would have stopped this collusion of thieves before it started. But this example illuminates the dangers of not properly controlling all elements of a cash system (not to mention the dangers of absentee ownership!).

## 12. Cash Control

Careful handling of cash assets is the backbone of all successful cost control systems. Cash, as opposed to any other type of asset, is the most obvious and safest thing for a thief to steal. Once the cash has been taken, the theft is a *fait acompli*. There is no second stage to the crime. No stolen goods have to be fenced, and no collusion between the back of the house and the front is necessary. Catching an employee leaving your restaurant with a chicken under his or her coat is catching a thief red-handed. Catching an employee with a pocketful of cash proves little.

Your managers or bookkeeper are not likely to steal from you (although they might), and most servers are honest. But you will have a large number of servers, and because these positions turn over frequently, the risk of theft or of careless cash handling is greater at these positions than at any other.

A good cash control system provides a clear paper trail of the chain of custody of cash, from the moment it is collected from the customer until it is deposited in your business's bank account. Cash control begins with the creation of proper cash-handling procedures, and service staff must understand clearly what is expected of them in this regard. Any violation by staff of the cash control procedures you set up must be seen as attempted theft and therefore as a firing offence.

If an old-fashioned, handwritten, guest-check system is used, with a cashier settling all cash payments from customers, the wait staff must understand that all money transactions, even making change, must be done through the cashier. The wait staff should be issued sequentially numbered guest checks that they are responsible for, and these must be reconciled with the cash receipts by the cashier at the shift's end. Doing so will prevent the staff from collecting money from a customer and simply keeping it and destroying the guest check.

If, as is more commonly the case these days, an electronic cash system (a point-of-sale system, or POS) is used, wait staff will accumulate the cash receipts themselves. Wherever possible, wait staff should not be able to gain access to product without first having rung it in. Similarly, the production staff must have access to the product but should not be allowed access to the customers. In this way, the wait staff cannot obtain any product without accounting for it through the POS system, and the production staff cannot convert product into cash by selling it directly to the customers. Any theft would require collusion between a front-of-house employee and a back-of-house employee, and the two together are more likely to eventually get caught.

Ringing in to the POS system should be the only way a server can order food from the kitchen or bar. Each server can access the POS system only with a key of some kind. This may be as simple as a secret server number, a swipe card, or an actual POS key. The key identifies the server to the POS system, which keeps track of all servers' transactions.

*Cost control* **181**

## 12.1  Cashing out

At the end of the shift the server must turn over all credit-card charges, house charges, and enough cash to cover the amount rung into the POS system. This procedure is commonly referred to as "cashing out."

Wait staff cash out by signing off, or "ringing out," of the POS system at the end of the shift using their personal POS keys. The manager, using a special management key, takes a "read" — a printout from the POS system that shows how much the individual servers have sold during the shift. The manager and each server together count the out the money the server owes to the house. Sometimes the sever will count out his or her money first, and then the manager will verify the count. The count is documented on a cash-out sheet, such as Sample 15, designed to show the amount owed and the means of payment (i.e., the various charge vouchers, travelers' checks, and cash tendered in each denomination of bill and coin). The POS printout is attached to the cash-out sheet, which the manager and the server both sign. The signing signifies that both parties agree on the amount of cash owed and paid and prevents any "adjustment" of the amounts after the cash out is completed. Cash outs should be done in a secure location, away from the public.

Bartender cash outs must be handled differently. Bartenders are the only servers who have access to both the product they are selling and the customers to whom they are selling it. If the bartender does not ring in the drink, or rings in an inaccurate amount, the loss of product or the inaccuracy of the ring in can be verified only by other inventory controls. To prevent such a situation, the actual cash collected must be reconciled with the cash that should have been collected according to the POS printout. The bartender must not be allowed to know what the printout total is until he or she has submitted all the cash collected. This way if product was not rung into the POS system but was sold and the money collected, the "overage" is still kept by the management until inventory controls can account for the discrepancy. A bartender's summary sheet, like the one in Sample 16, can also be useful in tracking the flow of product and cash.

## 12.2  Daily sales reconciliation

The reconciled cash-out sheets are, in fact, a paper trail of all cash collected from the various servers over the day. These cash-out sheets should be summarized on a daily sales summary sheet. Once the cash

**182**  *Start and run a restaurant business*

## Sample 15
# SERVER CASH-OUT SHEET

Day _____     Date _____

| SERVER | # | PREVIOUS BALANCE | VOIDS | CREDIT CARD ||| STAFF MEALS | HOUSE CHARGES | MISC. | CABH | INITIALS ||
|--------|---|------------------|-------|------|------|------|-------------|---------------|-------|------|------|------|
|        |   |                  |       | VISA | M.C. | AMEX |             |               |       |      | MGR. | EMP. |
|        |   |                  |       |      |      |      |             |               |       |      |      |      |
|        |   |                  |       |      |      |      |             |               |       |      |      |      |
|        |   |                  |       |      |      |      |             |               |       |      |      |      |
|        |   |                  |       |      |      |      |             |               |       |      |      |      |
|        |   |                  |       |      |      |      |             |               |       |      |      |      |
|        |   |                  |       |      |      |      |             |               |       |      |      |      |
|        |   |                  |       |      |      |      |             |               |       |      |      |      |
|        |   |                  |       |      |      |      |             |               |       |      |      |      |
|        |   |                  |       |      |      |      |             |               |       |      |      |      |
|        |   |                  |       |      |      |      |             |               |       |      |      |      |
|        |   |                  |       |      |      |      |             |               |       |      |      |      |
| TOTALS: |  |                  |       |      |      |      |             |               |       |      |      |      |

## Sample 16
## BARTENDER'S SUMMARY

___A.M. ___P.M.

Date_____  Day_____

|  | Opening Inventory | Adjustments | Closing Inventory | # of Bottles Sold | Tape Sales | Short | Over-ring | Total |
|---|---|---|---|---|---|---|---|---|
| Domestic bottles | | | | | | | | |
| Premium bottles | | | | | | | | |
| Import bottles | | | | | | | | |
| Domestic wine | | | | | | | | |
| Imported wine | | | | | | | | |
| House wine | | | | | | | | |
| Vintage wine | | | | | | | | |
| Tape sales | | | | | | | | |
| Total sales | | | | | | | | |
| Float | | | | | | | | |
| Cash total | | | | | | | | |
| Cash over/short | | | | | | | | |

**CASH**
**BILLS:** _____ X 100
_____ X 50
_____ X 20
_____ X 10
_____ X 5
_____ X 1
TOTAL: _____

**ROLLED COINS:**
_____ X .25     _____ X $ 1.
_____ X .10     _____ X $ 2.
_____ X .05
_____ X .01
TOTAL: _____

**LOOSE COINS:**
_____ X .25     _____ X $ 1.
_____ X .10     _____ X $ 2.
_____ X .05
_____ X .01
TOTAL: _____

**CASH:** _____
**EXPENSES:** _____

**EXPENSES:   (EXPLAIN)**

_____
_____
_____
_____
_____
_____
_____
_____
_____
_____

TOTAL: _____

**SIGNATURES:**
EMPLOYEE _____
MANAGER _____

outs are completed, place the cash itself in a locked safe. At the end of the day, make up the floats for the next day and deposit the cash from the day's sales into the company's bank account. For security's sake, the smaller the amount of cash kept on the premises the better. The bank-stamped deposit slip, along with all cash-out sheets with their POS printouts, should be attached to the daily sales summary sheet. Together, these provide the documentation that tracks the chain of custody of the cash from server to company's bank account.

## 12.3  Floats

Floats should contain only enough money to enable the cashier or bartender to make sufficient change throughout his or her shift. Therefore, floats should be made up of rolled coin and small bills, with the total amount depending on the volume of business expected during the shift. Floats should be composed of the same combination of rolled coin and small bills every day. Cashiers and bartenders can become very efficient at counting their floats if they know exactly how much and in what form the floats will be. They should count their floats directly upon receiving them and report any discrepancy to management immediately. It is normal operating procedure to charge an employee for any shortages at the end of their shift, and of course, if the float is short and the employee fails to report it, he or she will be charged for that shortage later.

**KEY POINT:** A simple means of testing the honesty and/or competence of a new employee is to add an extra $10 to his or her float and see if he or she reports it.

# 13. Till Procedures

Bartenders and cashiers must be trained in proper till procedures, just as they must be taught the proper protocols for ringing in to the POS system. Without proper training, an employee can make costly and time-consuming errors.

The till should always be set up in the same way. Most often, smaller denomination coins and bills are placed on the right. However, the actual choice of where the bills and coins go is not as important as always placing them in the same position, no matter who is working. This way, if a manager or other employee steps in to relieve a bartender, he or she will automatically know how the till is set up and will be able to make change with speed and accuracy.

If the till is part of the POS system, it will usually not open unless an item has been rung into the system. See that your bartenders know they must close the till drawer after each transaction. This practice will help prevent "no rings," in which the customer is served and change is made from the open till drawer, but the item sold is not rung in to the POS system. Ensuring that the bartender rings in all sales is probably the single most important step in effective cost control.

Anyone who has worked making change has heard the old line "But I gave you a twenty, not a ten" from some unhappy (or sometimes dishonest) customer. To prevent confusion, tell your staff to leave the bill being changed on the top of the money drawer until the customer has accepted his or her change. If a mistake has been made, the original bill proffered can still be distinguished from those already in the till.

Change given back to customers should be counted out. Never allow service staff to assume that any amount of change was meant to be kept as a gratuity.

## 13.1 *Pulling the till*

"Pulling the till" is a common technique that can ensure that a bartender rings in all the sales he or she makes. At any given time during a shift, the money in the till should equal the total sales plus the amount of the original float. Pulling the till is done by taking a "read" from the POS system to see how much has been rung in to that point. Then the till drawer, with all the cash, is taken from the bartender and replaced with a new till drawer with a new float, which allows the bartender to continue working. The cash in the original till drawer is compared to the "read" amount plus the float. If the amounts do not match, there is a good chance that the bartender has been "under ringing" in an attempt to keep some of the money for him or herself.

## 13.2 *Spotters*

Professional security people (called spotters) who are versed in the cash procedures your operation uses can be useful in ensuring that bartenders ring in all the product they sell. Spotters pose as customers and watch your service staff work. Naturally, a dishonest employee will be

**186**   *Start and run a restaurant business*

on his or her best behavior when a manager is near, but managers cannot always be watching. Spotters, however, often see an employee's "real" work habits.

Spotters can be used either on a random basis or to watch a particular employee. They can not only detect theft, but also observe how diligent, efficient, or customer-friendly employees are. They usually provide written reports, and can even testify in court if the situation leads to prosecution for theft or complaints of wrongful dismissal.

Often just the knowledge that spotters are being used on a random basis is enough to keep all but the most aggressive thief relatively honest.

## 13.3  Skims

Skims can be employed when high volume sales lead to a large build-up of a server's cash. A large amount of cash in a relatively exposed place, such as in a server's apron or in a bartender's till, is an invitation to robbery. To avoid such an occurrence, simply take money out of the till or from the wait staff during the shift and leave the server with a receipt, which he or she can exchange when cashing out.

## 13.4  Counterfeit money

All staff working with cash should be trained in the rudimentary elements of recognizing counterfeit bills. Using today's high-quality scanners and printers, even unskilled amateur counterfeiters can create a reasonable-looking fake. Counterfeit money is so common these days that many small businesses simply refuse to accept hundred– or even fifty-dollar bills.

Train your employees to feel for differences in paper quality. Office supply stores such as Business Depot or Staples sell inexpensive counterfeit felt pens, which cashiers can use to expose fake bills. Simply make a slash mark with the pen on either side of the face of the bill. If it's a fraud, dots will appear under the felt line.

If you need outside help in training your staff, often your local police department or even local financial institutions will provide seminars or videos on how to recognize counterfeit bills. Of course, such training must focus on the front-line staff, as it serves no purpose for managers to discover counterfeit money during cash out, long after the person who passed the bill has left the premises.

*Cost control*  **187**

# Chapter 14
# BARS AND PUBS

In many respects, bars and pubs differ little from restaurants in the way in which they are operated. Accounting, control, production, and service systems are similar in both types of operation. There are, however, some important distinctions.

In a restaurant, food is the primary product sold. Beverage alcohol, if sold at all, is a derived product. That is, customers usually go to a restaurant to eat, and alcoholic beverages — a cocktail or aperitif before dinner, wine with dinner, a brandy or liqueur after dinner — are an extension of the meal. The alcoholic beverage is directly related to the food ordered. But in bars and pubs, beverage alcohol is the primary product sold, and food is often a derived product. Although the local pub might serve excellent food and do a strong food business, patrons mostly go there for social reasons, rather than to dine.

Bars and pubs have a different target market than do restaurants. Customers go to the neighborhood bar or pub to be entertained, relax with friends, socialize, and meet new people. They might decide to eat while there, but dining is not their primary motivation. This chapter focuses on how to effectively market to the bar and pub crowd, and on how to meet their social and entertainment needs.

There are many types of establishments that serve beverage alcohol as a primary product, including bars, pubs, lounges, and clubs, and we would be foolhardy to attempt to address the many and varied operational differences in a book of this size and scope. We will concentrate here on small to mid-size bars and pubs that have many similarities to restaurants of the same size. Large scale bars, live-entertainment venues, dance clubs, band bars, and lounges are beyond the range of this book, and we will leave them for another time and place.

## 1. *Responsible Service of Alcohol*

The most obvious difference between the operation of a bar or pub and a restaurant is the focus on the service of alcohol. And the service of alcoholic beverages, while popular and profitable, presents the bar or pub owner/operator with certain challenges.

Alcohol is a potent drug. Used in moderation, it can be a wonderful social support. Used in excess, it can have serious and even tragic results. The bar/pub operator must walk a fine line: he or she should serve alcohol to customers to the point of facilitating pleasant social interaction, but must stop short of leaving them intoxicated. Intoxicated patrons may be incapable of reasonable judgment and may injure themselves and/or others.

Liquor laws are specific to each state and province. But the common-law precedent supporting the possible liability of a provider of alcohol is virtually universal to all jurisdictions in the United States and Canada. That means that the bar owner and employees can be held legally responsible for the actions of patrons that were served to the point of intoxication on their premises!

These days, courts are awarding damages in the millions of dollars to injured plaintiffs. A seemingly simple mistake by a bartender in serving a customer that last "one for the road" might lead to the loss of your business and even to personal bankruptcy.

Train your service staff in the responsible service of alcohol. This is not just a prudent step in risk management; it is essential. Many states and provinces have officially recognized programs or courses that you and your staff can take. The National Restaurant Association of America (on the Web at <www.restaurant.org/>), and in Canada, the Province of Ontario and the Province of British Columbia, to name but a few, have sponsored these types of training programs. The British Columbia initiative is called Serving It Right (check the Web at <www.servingitright.com>). The Ontario program is called Smart Serve (on the Web at <www.smartserve.ca>). The National Restaurant Association of America's Education Foundation has a responsible alcohol service program called Bar Code. You can find it on their Web site at <www.nraef.org>. You can obtain specific information about these programs by mail from your state or provincial licensing bodies or from the applicable Web sites.

## 2. *Handling Difficult Situations*

Some of the toughest situations with which bar staff and management must cope involve intoxicated customers. Sooner or later, all bar staff will have to face arguments. violence, or the difficult task of informing a customer who has become intoxicated that he or she is "cut off." Refusing to serve an intoxicated patron a drink can lead to a difficult, even dangerous confrontation.

In these situations, there are several steps you should take:

1. Be sure you know whose responsibility it is to approach the customer. Your house policy manual should make this clear. Many owners want this potentially risky job handled only by management.

2. Get backup. Never attempt to stop service or ask a customer to leave unless you have informed the management or other staff members of what you are doing, even if it is only to have the bartender watching from the bar. You may need physical help if the situation becomes violent or a witness if there is litigation in the future.

3. Identify yourself, particularly if you are not in uniform and have not been the table's regular server. You don't want an intoxicated patron, especially one who might be arguing with another customer, to mistake you for a friend of his or her "antagonist."

4. Be calm. Do not aggravate an already tense situation. Avoid raising your hands or "squaring off," which the intoxicated

*Bars and pubs* **191**

patron might construe as aggression. Do not touch the person. Be assertive, but speak calmly. Explain that service will be discontinued and that the customer should leave. State that you are simply following the house policy. Do not make it personal. You are simply doing your job.

5. Be discrete. Don't embarrass the patron in front of his friends. Speak to him privately, if possible. Perhaps you can even elicit help from the patron's more sober friends.

6. Remember, you have a duty in common law to keep the person from "foreseeable harm," such as driving under the influence, so if you think the patron is driving, arrange alternative transportation. Your establishment should have policies on how to handle this. Ask for the customer's car keys and offer to call a cab for him or her. You cannot make a patron comply with this; in fact, you cannot make any patron turn over private property to you. But you can warn him or her that you will inform the police if he or she insists on driving. If the patron will not leave or if violence seems imminent, tell him or her you will call the police. If the patron still does not comply, *make the call.* Calling the police may seem drastic when nothing untoward has actually happened; but remember, the criterion that would be used in any legal case that *might* develop if something nasty did happen is, "Was this foreseeable?" and "Did [your] staff behave 'reasonably' under the circumstances?" By calling the police, even if you only suspect the situation might get out of hand, you will be doing much more than just calling for a helping hand: you will be mitigating any charges that you did not take all "reasonable" steps possible to ensure the safety of your customers and staff.

7. After the patron has left, document the events in the manager's logbook or fill out the appropriate incident report forms. You have no way of knowing if you may be in court two years later trying to justify the decisions you have just made, so write down all the details, including the names and addresses of witnesses, while these things are still fresh in your memory.

8. If there is some question as to the effectiveness of your "house" policies (e.g., "How did the patron manage to get served to the point of intoxication in the first place?"), review the incident at the next management and/or staff meeting.

**192** *Start and run a restaurant business*

The same steps are involved when coping with other difficult situations, such as arguments or fights. The safety of your staff and your customers must always be your first concern. If you feel you cannot control the situation using the procedures listed above, you should call the police. You run the risk of being held liable for injuries to other customers or your own employees if you do not take reasonable measures to protect them in these circumstances.

# 3. Bar Service and Products

There are several differences in the service techniques used, as well as in the products served, in bars as opposed to restaurants.

## 3.1 Bar service

In a bar or pub, the service of food is a little less formal than it is in a restaurant. "Roll-ups" (knife and fork rolled up in a napkin) are often used instead of place settings. Food might be served to individuals in the same party at different times, rather than one course served to everyone at the table simultaneously, as is done in proper dining-room service. Another important difference in service styles is the "cash and carry" service of beverages. It is common practice, especially later in the evening after dinner service, for wait staff to bring rounds to customers who simply pay cash for them directly rather than running a tab, which is the normal procedure for food service in restaurants.

Cash-and-carry service presents some control problems. The paper trail of inventory from purchasing to sale (see chapter 13, "Cost Control") now stops with the wait staff rather than the customer. Therefore, one of the checks and balances that prevent wait staff from overcharging the customer is gone: no bill is presented that the customer can check against the menu to verify how much he or she should be paying. And often the hectic environment of a busy bar discourages customers from questioning what they might feel is a slightly "enlarged" bill. Watchful management and the use of spotters are the only effective remedies for this problem. Neighborhood pubs with a high number of regulars are somewhat immune, as the regulars frequently have a good idea of what the prices are.

*Bars and pubs*  **193**

## 3.2 Bar products

### 3.2a Spirits

Naturally, bars and pubs carry a greater variety of alcoholic beverages than restaurants. Promotional use of products such as "beer from around the world" or "200 varieties of single-malt scotch" is a common method for attracting customers, but a few words of caution regarding bar inventories are in order. Alcoholic-beverage inventories turn over much slower than food inventories. It is not unusual to have certain varieties of liquor that sell only a few shots a month. Remember that having excessive money tied up in inventory for long periods of time is poor business practice. The money invested in those 200 varieties of scotch does not earn you any profit until the scotch is sold. It is often the case that you must pay C.O.D. for these products (and in Canada, the government controls the sale of beverage alcohol and does not offer terms or discounts on purchases). Be sure that the customer response to any marketing strategy involving large inventories will be strong enough to justify the amount of capital you'll have tied up in it.

You will probably need to carry a case or two of each of the bar, or "well," brands (inexpensive base spirits used to make most highballs and cocktails). Vodka, gin, rum, tequila, scotch, and rye are the usual bar spirits, depending on the local market's preferences. You might stock several premium, or "call," brands of each of these as well. And don't forget the 20 or 30 various types of liqueurs or cordials that you will also carry to use in certain cocktails. It is not unusual to have several thousand dollars invested in liquor inventory!

### 3.2b Beer

Beer is often the best-selling alcoholic beverage. In addition, there are many other benefits for the bar owner in selling beer, especially draft (draught) beer. Beer is, in most instances, less expensive than other alcoholic beverages, and draft beer usually has a better profit margin than bottled beer. Draft beer can be served in several glass sizes to attract various customers: small glasses for those who are "samplers," 12-ounce steins for those who want more, 20-ounce British pints for the serious beer drinkers, and even pitchers for groups.

Modern consumers are becoming more and more interested in microbrewery products in addition to the old standbys from the large breweries (Anhauser-Busch in the USA, and Molson and Labatt in

Canada). Beware though: specialty beers may provide marketing opportunities, but they also require more care in handling. Unpasteurized draft beer has a short shelf life (28 days) compared to bottled beer (3 to 4 months) and must be kept refrigerated and served under pressure through clean, well-maintained equipment.

Be certain you plan your beverage menu well in advance of opening. Unforeseen design, construction, and storage problems might prevent you from easily adding the necessary equipment to sell certain beverages; for instance, draft beer, should you decide as an afterthought, to add it to your beverage menu.

### 3.2c Wine

Wine is frequently the poorest-selling alcoholic beverage in bars. Often having a choice of one or two house whites and the same number of house reds by the glass will suffice, depending on the market and your own style of operation.

**KEY POINT:** Co-author Brian Floody's experience operating bars and pubs in the 1980s and 1990s yielded some interesting information on beer versus wine sales. It was unusual for wine sales to surpass even 5 percent of the total beverage sales, whereas beer often accounted for more than 70 percent.

### 3.2d Bar food

Bar food — "pub grub," or whatever term you prefer for food meant to be served to bar customers — should be as carefully planned as your beverage menu. Even though your food sales may account for less than 20 percent or 30 percent of your overall sales, it is crucial that the product be good. When planning your bar menu, keep in mind that you should serve items that your customers can easily consume while standing. Quesadillas, buffalo-style chicken wings, and other finger food make good choices.

One of the paradoxes of the bar business is that you will spend more time and energy on your poorest-selling product (food) because people will remember your bar more for the food then the drinks. A beer served at your bar is exactly the same as that brand of beer served at the bar next door, but your food gives you the chance to demonstrate your uniqueness and superiority over your competitors.

## 4. Bar Equipment and Small Wares

Bars should be designed and equipped with great care and forethought, as often a busy bar will account for the majority of the bar or pub's business. The bar equipment you will need to acquire will depend on the specific production requirements of your beverage menu. However, bar menu items tend to be similar enough that a *generic* list of equipment, small wares, and condiments, such as the one presented below, might be of value. This list is not exhaustive, and naturally your own preferences and market's expectations might lead you to modify it.

### 4.1 Bar equipment

Pouring stations — the designated areas behind the bar where the bartender stands to take orders — should be designed so bartenders need make only the minimum number of steps to produce and serve your full beverage menu. Therefore, the placement of the following equipment must be carefully considered. The use of an experienced consultant or facilities designer at this stage can often substantially increase the efficiency of a busy bar.

☞ **Refrigeration:** Several types of bar refrigeration are available depending on your needs. Back-bar "lowboys" with counter space on top are popular for bottled beer, as are tall, glass-doored, pop-cooler-style refrigerators. Glass chillers (to put a frost film on beer glasses) and self-contained icemakers can also be located behind the bar if space and/or volume of business allow. Stand-alone, self-contained refrigerators are popular, but we recommend remote compressors, if space allows, as they do not use up valuable inches in the bar and are generally more economical to run and easier to access for service.

☞ **Draft beer taps:** Either with single- or double-keg cooling units or connected to remote keg rooms, which is best if you intend to have several varieties of draft beers available.

☞ **Soft-drink dispensers:** Pre- or post-mix pop dispensers with tower and/or gun dispensers for large-volume sales (bottled or canned pop takes up large amounts of room and requires a great deal of labor-intensive handling).

**196**  *Start and run a restaurant business*

☞ **Glass washers:** Automatic glass-washing equipment, kept behind the bar for smaller operations. If you expect a high volume of sales, the equipment should be accessible to both bar *and* floor staff.

☞ **Cash register or POS terminal:** Essential for control purposes for any degree of volume sales.

☞ **Entertainment equipment:** Controls for TVs, sound systems, and satellite hookups. Various board games that customers can use are often kept behind the bar.

☞ **Sinks:** Hand sinks with hot and cold running water are often required by health authorities for sanitation reasons. Three-compartment glass-washing sinks may be an alternative to automatic glass washers.

☞ **Blenders**: If your menu includes blended "frozen" cocktails, a blender or two will be the most economical solution. If you anticipate a large volume of business in this type of drink, it may be worthwhile for you to invest in a special "slushy" machine.

☞ **Speed rails:** Mounted on the underbar in front of the bartender for efficient service of often-used spirits and mixes. A speed rail is nothing more than a long bottle rack that is hung in front of the bartender at waist level so that drinks can be made quickly without the bartender having to turn around and reach for liquor bottles from the back bar display. The well brands of the basic spirits and the basic juices and mixes are kept in the speed rail.

☞ **Liquor display:** Usually behind the bartender on the back bar. It can be both a décor item and a merchandising tool for presenting your liqueurs and premium brands to the public.

☞ **Coffee machine:** Optional, but necessary if your establishment will offer a selection of coffee drinks.

## 4.2 *Small wares*

Small wares are essential to smooth service of beverage alcohol. The following are some of the basic items you should acquire before opening your bar or pub:

☞ ice scoops (Faster than tongs. Never allow your staff to use glassware or their hands to serve ice.)

*Bars and pubs* **197**

☞ bottle openers (Even with the proliferation of twist-off caps, these are necessary to open various imported beers.)

☞ can openers

☞ corkscrews (Lever action are best.)

☞ stainless steel shakers and mixing glasses

☞ spring strainers for cocktail shakers

☞ cocktail or "martini" stirring spoons

☞ pouring spouts for bottles

☞ various containers for spices and juices

☞ cutting board and paring knife to prepare garnishes

☞ garnish trays or containers to hold cut-fruit garnishes, etc.

☞ index card catalogue box or Rolodex for your cocktail recipes, or even a standard bar recipe book (There are many: *The Boston Bar Guide* and the *Barman's Bible* are examples of well-known ones.)

☞ lime squeezers, lemon peelers, zesters, glass rimmer, glass- and bottle-cleaning brushes, depending on your bar setup

☞ ice picks and ice chippers, if uncubed ice is used

## 4.3 *Disposable goods*

There are a number of disposable goods you should keep on hand:

☞ swizzle sticks

☞ straws (8" soda-fountain length, and 4" to 6" cocktail size)

☞ cocktail toothpicks or "swords" (for martini olives and maraschino cherries)

☞ miniature cocktail umbrellas or similar items to garnish specialty drinks

☞ cocktail napkins to protect bar finishes (can also be used as a marketing tool: print your logo and sales information on them)

*or*

☞ coasters (often donated by a liquor or beer supplier)

## 4.4  Bar condiments and juices

There are a great number of pre-prepared products on the market that may be used: various cocktail mixes both in powder and liquid form; for example, pina colada or mint julep ingredient mixes that need only have the appropriate alcoholic beverages added. In addition, be sure to always have the following available:

- ☞ angostura bitters
- ☞ Worchester Sauce
- ☞ Tabasco Sauce
- ☞ grenadine syrup (non-alcoholic sweetener)
- ☞ salt and pepper (nutmeg, cinnamon, and other spices are other options)
- ☞ orange juice, lemon and lime juices or a lemon/lime combination
- ☞ grapefruit, pineapple, tomato, and Clamato (in Canada) juices (optional, depending on the extensiveness of your cocktail offerings)

## 4.5  Garnishes

What cocktail would be complete without an appropriate garnish?

- ☞ oranges, lemons, and limes (cut into slices or wedges; standard garnish fruit, although many other types of fruit may be used)
- ☞ cocktail olives
- ☞ maraschino cherries

Cocktail (Gibson) onions, cocktail wieners, gerkins, and jalapeno peppers can also be used.

# 5.  Glassware

There is a wide variety of specialty glassware available, and there are some basic guidelines to bear in mind when purchasing it. Ask yourself these questions:

- ☞ *Is the glass the right size?* Does the drink recipe you plan to use fit into the glass?

☞ *Does the glassware suit your concept and your clientele's expectations?* Beer mugs are fine in a pub but maybe a little 'down market' for a fine-dining restaurant.

☞ *Is the glass durable enough to survive the amount of handling your volume of business will require?* Automatic glass washers can be deadly on small liqueur and sherry glasses and certain types of tall elegant glasses.

☞ *Is it affordable?* You will be replacing a certain amount of glassware continually, so be sure you have budgeted for it.

☞ *Is it replaceable?* It can be very frustrating to attempt to order more stock, only to find that the line you have selected as your house glassware has been discontinued. Be sure you can get replacement stock when you make your initial choices.

☞ *Do you have adequate storage?* You will need to store your glassware behind the bar in a place where the bartender can easily access it.

The following are some standard sizes and types of glassware:

☞ beer glasses (Ten-ounce, 12-ounce, and 20-ounce British pints are popular sizes in Pilsner, hourglass, sleeve, and mug or stein styles.)

☞ wineglasses (The ubiquitous "Paris goblet" is the most commonly used style of wineglass for bars. Neither too large for white wine nor too small for red wine, it usually does well for bar use and comes in a variety of sizes. Four- to six-ounce sherry glasses will be needed if port or sherry is offered. Don't forget snifters if you are planning to serve brandy.)

☞ water glass (Usually 12 ounces in a wide variety of styles.)

You will also need various spirit and cocktail glasses:

☞ high ball (eight to ten ounce)

☞ sling or zombie glass (12 ounce)

☞ collins glass (12 ounce)

☞ rocks or old-fashioned glass (eight to ten ounce)

☞ martini glass (Three- to five-ounce specialty large martini glasses can be used for signature martinis.)

- 👉 cocktail glass (three to six ounce)
- 👉 sour glass (four to five ounce)
- 👉 liqueur or pony glass (one to two ounce)
- 👉 shooter glass (one ounce)
- 👉 shot glass (measuring glass, usually marked at 1, 1¼, 1½ ounce)
- 👉 mixing glass (to go with a stainless steel shaker, usually 12 to 14 ounce)

There are also a large number of popular styles used for specialty drinks: viva grande, tulip, and hurricane glasses, to name but a few popular styles.

# 6. Control Systems

Chapter 13, "Cost Control," discussed the sensitivity of the bartender's position. The bartender has access to both the product and the customers to whom he sells it, and only rigorously enforced control procedures can ensure that all bar product will be sold and the full amount of money received for it will end up in the till. Again, we must emphasize the need to ensure that all sales are rung into the cash system. If the bartender must ring in all sales, many of the various methods used to steal at the bar are nullified.

For example, consider a common type of bar theft: a bartender simply sells liquor he or she has brought in and keeps the profit. A bartender buys a 40-ounce bottle of vodka for, let's say, $30, and sells off the 40 shots for $4 each. He or she has realized a profit of $130 (40 X $4 = $160, minus the original investment of $30 = $130). However, if all drinks must be rung into the POS system, the $160 in sales would have to be paid to the house at cash out, thereby nullifying the point of the theft. Similarly, the old bartender's trick of watering down the vodka and gin to be able to sell more is a pointless exercise if the bartender must ring in the "extra" sales, which would prevent him or her from keeping the extra money.

The easiest and most common means of bar theft is simply to ring in less then what is actually sold. For instance, a bartender is asked for four beers. The bartender serves four beers, collects for four beers, but rings in only three. The bartender keeps track of these "under rings"

*Bars and pubs* **201**

until he or she can take the "extra" cash out of the till. (This is sometimes called "building a bank.")

Of course, the trick is to enforce the requirement for all sales to be rung in, and as stated earlier, you should use a variety of control techniques to see that this is done. The most effective ways to prevent a bartender from building a bank are random spotting and occasionally pulling the till (see chapter 13 for more information on both methods).

## 6.1 *Mechanical controls*

Another very effective way to control theft in a busy bar is the use of mechanical controls. By mechanical controls, we mean the measurement and even the dispensing of alcoholic beverages by mechanical or electronic means. There are mechanical "exact pour" speed spouts available for liquor bottles that will automatically measure the standard amount of liquor in a standard portion. Even more sophisticated are electronic dispensing systems that not only measure exact portions, but do so through a computer-controlled, service-efficient "gun," so that the bartender does not even have access to the liquor bottles. You can also obtain electronic draft meters that measure the exact number of ounces that pass through a draft tap over a shift. And these are only a few examples of mechanical controls!

Not so long ago, mechanical controls such as electronic liquor-dispensing systems were too expensive for small bar or pub operators to even consider purchasing. But with the remarkable proliferation of computer technology in recent years, computer-run, automatic pouring systems have become more and more affordable. Mechanical control systems have many advantages, some obvious and some less so. Take the example of the automatic liquor dispenser. First and foremost, such a device will ensure consistency. An automatic pouring system will dispense an exact measure every time it is used. The service is fast, especially with a pouring gun with which several different liquors can be poured just by touching different buttons — no searching the back bar for that misplaced bottle! Control is also greatly improved. A bartender cannot tamper with the product, which is usually kept in a separate, locked area. An automatic pouring system can record every shot the bartender pours; sometimes these systems can even be integrated with your POS system, so that pouring the shot automatically rings in the drink itself. Less obvious is the substantial saving in time and energy in training bar staff. A liquor-dispensing system is easy to operate and requires less preparation then a "free pour" liquor setup.

**202** *Start and run a restaurant business*

But mechanical systems also have disadvantages. Any time you consider implementing any system of control, make a careful analysis of its cost/benefit ratio. The cost/benefit ratio compares the resources that would be expended to put the controls in place to the amount of revenue that would be saved by having the controls. Any form of control will cost something, even if it is only more of your own time. If you have a small bar operation, and your accounting practices show that your actual profit margins vary little from your target profit margins, you must carefully examine what is to be gained by spending several thousand dollars on equipment that might provide only a small decrease in that variation. A large club with high-volume liquor sales can easily justify the expense of an electronic liquor-dispensing system. A percentage of the revenue often lost by theft or overpouring as well as the increase in the speed of service will quickly pay for the initial cost of installation. However, it may take years for a small neighborhood pub to make back enough to pay for the initial investment.

You should also consider the less tangible effects of an automatic system. Perhaps your customers like the feeling of getting a slightly "heavier" shot from their favorite bartender. A good bartender can often appear to be pouring more than is actually ending up in the glass. And even if the regular shots are truly a little "heavy," the extra cost this incurs might be money well spent if it encourages your customers to return to your bar. Patrons of large clubs are often young and are mostly interested in getting their drinks quickly and socializing with their friends, whereas patrons of neighborhood pubs may drop in specifically to enjoy a leisurely drink and a chat with their favorite bartender.

The use of an automatic liquor dispenser can also mean the loss of the show that a good bartender can put on. Shaking a cocktail with a juggler's flair can be an enjoyable performance for customers to watch and is a traditional marketing tool. Dispense with it only if the control benefits are clearly obvious.

Regardless of these concerns, the judicious use of some mechanical controls is now the industry norm. The metering of draft lines is an example of the effective and unobtrusive use of mechanical controls (the meters can be placed under the bar or even in the draft cooler). These meters provide an excellent means of reconciling the beer actually used with the beer rung in to the POS system.

*Bars and pubs* **203**

## 7. Entertainment

As mentioned at the beginning of this chapter, one of the primary reasons people patronize bars is to be entertained. A bar or pub naturally should provide a variety of types of entertainment, such as big-screen TVs in sports bars, or various forms of music: tapes, CDs, juke boxes, DJs, or live bands. Or a bar may provide the means by which the customers can entertain themselves: pool tables, darts, video games, or interactive games like NTN football and trivia. You can also entertain your customers by running promotional events, parties, and contests to keep them interested and coming back for more.

Many of these entertainment systems, such as sound systems and TVs, can be purchased or leased. Others, such as pool tables, video games, and interactive TV games, can be contracted from outside suppliers on a profit-share basis. You can hire live entertainment directly or through booking agents. But no matter what type of entertainment you plan to provide, the question you must always ask and answer first is, "What costs are associated with this entertainment?" Spend a little time and energy researching *all* the costs attached to various types of entertainment.

Unfortunately, however, some of these costs are not immediately apparent. For example, suppose you decide to put in dartboards or pool tables because you believe that you can attract league players on slower weeknights. You must not only research how much purchasing or leasing the equipment itself would be, but also consider the number of seats and amount of floor space you will have to give up (and the revenue they bring in) to accommodate these games. If you have enough space and are sure there is plenty of interest, dartboards or pool tables may be excellent additions to your bar, but always be sure you understand all the costs, both direct and indirect.

Another example is hiring a live band. Perhaps you can negotiate paying the band a percentage of the revenue that they can attract over and above a regular night. Or you can pay them with a "door" charge. But don't forget you may have to rent a PA sound system or put up better lighting. There might be printing costs for door passes and advertising flyers and posters, as well as labor costs for someone to be stationed at the door. There may also be intangible costs, such as complaints from your neighbors about noise levels.

Be sure you calculate all the associated costs of the entertainment so you can accurately judge whether an increase in revenue will mean an actual increase in bottom-line profit.

# 8. Advertising and Promotion

Marketing is an ongoing process. Understanding your customers' interests and needs is only the first step. You must then make your customers aware that your establishment can meet their needs and even exceed their expectations. You can accomplish this task by means of advertising, promotional strategies, and public relations.

## 8.1 Advertising

The best advertising for most bars, like restaurants, is word of mouth, but bars have to work especially hard to keep their customers' attention. This involves developing an ongoing media advertising campaign (see chapter 12, "Marketing").

When you first open your bar or pub, the main purpose of your advertising will be to inform the public of your existence and to persuade them to come in. Inviting the local newspaper down to have a look at your establishment just before you open might garner you some free coverage in the entertainment or restaurant sections. However, in most instances you will need to pay for some well-placed and well-timed advertising in the local media to focus the attention of your target customers on your establishment. We prefer the "soft" style of opening, rather than the large, well-publicized type of grand opening that so often only showcases the new staff's inability to cope with a very busy first night. Better to quietly open your doors and let business build slowly, and then have an "official" opening party a few weeks later, once your staff have practiced working together and are better prepared to cope with a busy night.

Once you are up and running, you will use advertising not just to inform and persuade people to give your establishment a try, but also to remind your old customers that your bar or pub is still a fun place to go — to keep you establishment "positioned" in the market, to use the now-familiar jargon. For bars, it is frequently more effective to advertise a specific event, rather than rely on a general information message. Ongoing promotional events will give you something specific and new on which to focus your advertising.

*Bars and pubs* **205**

## 8.2 Promotional strategies

Restaurants can advertise and promote their chefs and their menus. After all, people go to a restaurant primarily to eat. Bars, however, need to create the sense that there is always something entertaining happening at their venue. An ongoing series of events can achieve this. These events may be repeated regularly or may be one-time-only affairs; for instance, a Super Bowl party to take advantage of the enormous promotional hype surrounding the game, or a weekly trivia contest or dart tournament so that customers will book a weekly night out at your bar. Or you might hire a jazz trio to play on Sunday afternoons to build up revenue during this traditionally slow time. Whatever events you decide to run, be certain to create them with the interests of your target market in mind. There is little point in having a jazz trio play on Sundays if your clientele is primarily interested in country music.

A promotion summary form can be of great help when developing these events. This form is used to record information needed when creating special events, and can act both as a checklist (so that you can be certain you haven't overlooked a crucial step in the development process) and as a reference document that you can review to see what succeeded at previous promotions and what did not. It can be extremely useful to review the summary forms from past events when developing annual promotions, such as a New Year's Eve or Halloween party.

Such a summary form should contain the following information:

1.  *What are the goals of your promotion?*

    What do you expect to achieve? Is the promotion designed to make money? To introduce a new product? To attract a slightly different type of customer (e.g., jazz lovers on Sunday afternoons)?

2.  *What activities will take place during the event?*

    Will there be contests? Door prizes? Entertainment? Special food or drinks?

    Be sure to include all your staff in these decisions. Some of the best ideas will come from your employees, who often have more direct contact with your customers than you do. Also, the more involved your employees are in developing a promotional event, the better they will be at "selling it" to your customers beforehand and at enthusiastically participating in the event itself.

3. *What resources will be needed?*

If you are promoting a new product, do you have enough of it? Will the product's supplier sponsor or support your promotional event? Do you have enough glassware, china, flatware to effectively serve the new product? If you are going to have contests, who will run these? Do you have enough staff scheduled? What will the prizes be? Can you get prizes donated, or will you have to budget for them? Work out the logistics of the promotion from start to finish so you can establish the resources — human and material — that you will need.

4. *Design an effective advertising campaign.*

Far too often, we have gone to wonderfully entertaining promotions that were not well attended because not enough time and money were spent advertising them to the target market. No matter how exciting the promotion is, it will not have the desired effect if the market it was designed to impress doesn't attend because they didn't find out about it!

If you are running a variety of interesting events, use the entertainment listings in your local media to advertise them. This is a good way to get your bar some press or air time, and it's often free. And don't neglect other methods for getting your message to the market. See chapter 12, "Marketing," for more information.

5. *Do a complete budget.*

How much will the event cost to run and how much do you anticipate in revenue from the event? Don't forget those "hidden" costs like the extra busboy you bring in to help clean up.

You shouldn't always expect to make a profit. Naturally, most events are designed to make money — the jazz trio on Sundays, for instance — but you may want to do other events for different reasons, such as a Christmas party to thank your regular customers for their patronage. In all cases, however, you must understand exactly what the event will cost you before proceeding. This is especially important for promotional events that might have long-term, residual costs, such as a two-for-one coupon advertising campaign. The coupons may continue to appear for months after the event is over!

6.   *Evaluate the promotion's effectiveness.*

Evaluating a promotion can be more difficult than you'd think. Often, though, two or three techniques can be used. The first and easiest is to look at the sales figures. Be careful not to assume that all the revenue taken in on the night of the promotion was generated solely by the promotion. If the bar would have been open for business in any case, then only the revenue over and above that for the average night should be attributed to the event.

It is more difficult to assess the intangible advertising value of customers describing the enjoyable time they had to others. In addition, don't overlook the obvious if somewhat subjective evaluation method of asking staff and customers for their feedback, either by comment cards or in direct conversation. Write down your own impressions as well. We suggest even having a post-mortem discussion at the next manager's meeting, so that all suggestions regarding what worked and what didn't can be recorded on your form and kept on file.

The main purpose of promotional events, of course, is to convey the impression that there is "always something going on down at _____ [your bar]." The idea is to have your bar's name pop into the mind of anyone in your chosen market segment who wants to go out, but doesn't quite know where he or she feels like going.

## 8.3 Public relations

Public relations is often the best tactic for getting your establishment some high-profile and unbiased attention in the media. It's important for you to see to it that your establishment is perceived by your neighbors as a positive part of the community. Remember that you will always have to combat some of the negative feelings about alcohol that are present in any community (especially if there has been a local drunk-driving incident or something similar in the recent past).

You can defeat those negative stereotypes by ensuring that you are perceived as a good community citizen. Sponsoring a local sports team is a good way to garner favor. But sponsor local kids' teams too, not just the adult softball team whose members promise to come to your establishment for a beer after the game. Your neighbors will respond with their patronage.

Linking a special promotional event to fund-raising for a local charity is another good way to build your image as a responsible member of the community. Suppliers and customers alike are far more forthcoming with money for that annual golf tournament or a similar event when they feel they are helping a good cause too.

A friend of co-author Gina McNeill's promotes a charity pub crawl every year in "Old Cabbage Town" in Toronto. As many as 70 people pay $20 to sign up to travel along as a group (or two groups, depending on the numbers) to several different bars and pubs in the area. Each bar participates by offering the group appetizers or small munchies for free and putting on something interesting or exciting (entertainment, music, or special food). The "crawlers" must buy a ticket and are responsible for their own drinks. The bars get the exposure to new prospective customers, usually some coverage in the local paper and, of course, the beverage revenue. The customers have a pleasant evening out, partying through the quaint old neighborhood. The charity raises some money, and a good time is had by all.

Public relations, like good promotions and effective advertising, is an on-going challenge that must be constantly addressed.

Whether you are planning to operate a restaurant or a small bar or pub, the key to success is your understanding of the people who make up your target market. Discover what their needs and wants are, and then provide for these — and ensure that your market knows about it.

Now that you've finished reading this book, use Checklist 7 to evaluate your skills and ability to successfully open your restaurant or bar. Consider the following tasks, and identify those areas in which you may need support from outside sources.

## Checklist 7
# ANALYZE YOUR READINESS TO START AND RUN YOUR RESTAURANT OR BAR

| Task | Self/Team | Consultant | Take a course | Date completed |
|---|---|---|---|---|
| Business plan | | | | |
| Feasibility study | | | | |
| Capital budgeting | | | | |
| Permits and licenses | | | | |
| Menu development | | | | |
| Marketing plan | | | | |
| Advertising campaign | | | | |
| Design and layout | | | | |
| Lighting | | | | |
| Renovation/contracting | | | | |
| Purchasing | | | | |
| Food and liquor | | | | |
| Equipment | | | | |
| Small wares | | | | |
| Furniture | | | | |
| China and glassware | | | | |
| Uniforms | | | | |
| POS system | | | | |

# Conclusion

Congratulations if you have decided to pursue your dream. We hope that you have found the material in this book to be useful. Of all the information we have offered here, if we had to recommend a *must* do before opening your restaurant, it would be to complete your feasibility study and business plan and take a very hard look at your business structure. If your structure includes a partner or partners, then, with the help of *independent* legal counsel, work out a formal partnership agreement. This piece of advice alone could save you much anguish years from now. Partnerships gone bad are probably as much to blame for the high failure rate in restaurants as undercapitalization is.

After that, take care of your staff. Treat them fairly. Provide incentives for them when they exceed your standards and support their growth through training. Listen to your customers. Stay positive and respond to their new and ever-changing demands.

With this advice we hope we will help you realize your dream and enjoy the daily challenges that you will face as the master of your own fate and a "master of ceremonies" to all!

# Selected Bibliography

Coltman, Michael, and Martin Jagels. *Hospitality Management Accounting.* 8th ed. New York: Wiley, 2003.

Dittmer, Paul. *Principles of Food, Beverage, and Labor Cost Controls.* 7th ed. New York: Wiley, 2002.

Dorf, Martin E. *Restaurants That Work.* New York: Whitney Library of Design, Watson-Guptil Publishing, 1992.

Foulkes, Christopher, ed. *Larousse Pocket Encyclopedia of Wine.* Paris: Larousse, 1996.

Johnson, Hugh, and Jancis Robinson. *The World Atlas of Wine.* New York: Mitchell Beazley, 2001.

Katsigris, Costas, Mary Porter, and Chris Thomas. *The Bar and Beverage Book.* 3rd ed. New York: Wiley, 2002.

Katz, Jeff B. *Restaurant Planning, Design, and Construction.* New York: Wiley, 1997.

Keister, Douglas. *Food and Beverage Control.* 2nd ed. Upper Saddle River, NJ: Pearson Education, 1996.

LeFever, Michael M. *Restaurant Reality: A Manager's Guide.* New York: Wiley, 1988.

Lipinski, Bob, and Kathie Lipinski. *Professional Beverage Management.* New York: Wiley, 1996.

Lovelock, Christopher H., and Jochen Wirtz. 5th ed. Upper Saddle River, NJ: Prentice Hall, 2003.

Ojugo, Clement. *Practical Food and Beverage Cost Control*. New York: Thomson Delmar Learning, 1998.

Robinson, Jancis. *Jancis Robinson's Guide to Wine Grapes*. New York: Oxford University Press, 1996.

Scanlon, Nancy Loman. *Quality Restaurant Service Guaranteed: A Training Outline*. New York: Wiley, 1998.

Stefanelli, John. *The Sale and Purchase of Restaurants*. 2nd ed. New York: Wiley, 1990.

Walton, Stuart. *Complete Guide to Wines and Wine Drinking*. London: Southwater, 2004.

Wilson, Tony. *Buying a Franchise in Canada*. Vancouver: Self-Counsel Press, 2004.